P9-AFS-508

GODLESS AND FREE

PAT CONDELL
GODLESS AND FREE

Copyright © Pat Condell 2010

All Rights Reserved. No part of this publication may be
reproduced or transmitted in any form or by any means,
electronic or mechanical, including photocopy, recording or
any other information storage and retrieval system, without
prior permission in writing from the author.

First published in 2010 by www.lulu.com

ISBN: 978-1-4452-2315-5

www.patcondell.net

Contents

Introduction

A number of people have asked for this book, so here it is. It contains the transcripts of sixty video monologues I posted on the internet between February 2007 and October 2009 because that's the only place they had a hope in hell of being seen.

I've been trying to say this stuff for years in the traditional media, but criticising religion is frowned on in ultra-sensitive multicultural Britain, especially at the BBC, so I had to be content with talking about it in comedy clubs and fringe theatres until I discovered internet video.

Early in 2007 I was looking for ways to publicise my show, *Faith Hope & Sanity – A few jokes about religion before it kills us all*, when I found something called *The Blasphemy Challenge*, an atheist campaign that invited people to make a short video of themselves denying the holy spirit (the only unforgivable sin) to show they weren't afraid of hellfire.

It seemed like a fun idea, so I made a video in my garden shed and posted it on YouTube. I didn't expect much to come of it, other than perhaps persuading a few people to come and see the show, and I was surprised and delighted to see it rack up thousands of hits in the first few days.

I realised this was a medium I should investigate further, so I made another video, *Hello America*, which had similar success, and it dawned on me that I could reach far more people like this than by poncing around in small theatres night after night, so I decided to ditch the show and focus on the internet.

Five and a half hours of video and thirty million hits later I'm still grateful for the chance to speak my mind to a wider audience without being censored. The novelty hasn't yet worn off, and so far I've been able to say what I like without interference, although with some censure.

The Trouble with Islam caused a minor ripple in Berkeley, California, in May 2007 when members of the local "Peace and Justice Commission" (I kid you not) condemned it as racist hate speech, which, in retrospect, and given that it was Berkeley, I've decided to take as a compliment.

Also, I fell foul of YouTube's notorious flagging policy in October 2008 when they removed *Welcome to Saudi Britain* for hate speech, because in it I call the country of Saudi Arabia mentally ill, which it very definitely is (and that's being kind).

However, hundreds of YouTube users responded by uploading the video to their own accounts, flooding the site with it. When the National Secular Society (of which I am a member) added its voice to the protest, the press picked up the story, whereupon YouTube promptly reinstated the video. Since then I've had no problems (though my videos are blocked in Dubai, I'm told).

I've tried to be as reasonable as I can in these videos, but when dealing with religion we're faced with the unreasonable, the intolerant, the outlandish and the preposterous, so, if you detect a certain harshness of tone, put it down to the fact that you can't cut through granite with an ordinary drill.

In other words, polite debate and respectful dialogue are wasted on religion, and if that's what you've come here for you're in the wrong place.

Godless and free is what I want to be. I don't think it's too much to ask, but, even if it is, I'm asking anyway, and I'm not taking no for an answer.

I don't expect everyone to agree with me. I know some atheists dislike my videos because they find them too insulting, and we'll have to agree to differ on that, as I don't think it's possible to be too insulting to a religious fundamentalist – though I'm always willing to try.

Others tell me I shouldn't refer to religion as mental illness, as it demeans people with real mental problems. Well, I think religious people have real mental problems. If you go through life thinking there's something wrong with you because of what Adam and Eve did six thousand years ago, then you're right, there is something wrong with you – it's called religion.

Most of the mail I get is very positive (though inevitably some isn't, as you can see on my website) and I'm grateful for everyone's support.

Christians generally agree with me about Islam, while wanting to put me right about God and Jesus. Some Muslims tell me I'm right to speak out against Islamism, while others call me a racist.

To the white supremacists I'm a race traitor. You can't win them all, I guess.

Also, I get a fair amount of abuse from left wing members of the multicultural appeasement lobby who are as blindly religious in their convictions as the Islamist nutcases they support.

These noble egalitarians don't see any irony in making common cause with misogynistic homophobic anti-Semites because they happen to share a virulent hatred of America, yet they seem to expect their opinions to be taken seriously – it's quite amazing.

In *Apologists for Evil* I explain how these clowns have poisoned my political outlook and helped to ensure that, though my leftish liberal views are still fairly intact, I'll never vote for a left wing party again.

As for religion, it goes without saying that I believe all gods are imaginary, all prophets are false, and all scriptures are lies.

I also believe that getting your morals from religion is like getting health advice from a tobacco company, and allowing religious sensibilities (especially Islamic ones) to censor free opinion is cultural suicide.

In a nutshell, freedom is my religion and the god of the desert is my Satan. Non-submission, heresy and blasphemy are my sacraments, and anyone who's offended by that can drop dead.

I hope you enjoy this book. In making a video, I prepare what I'm going to say in the same way I would a comedy routine, so how it comes out depends on the moment (no, I don't read from a teleprompter – thanks for asking); therefore some of this stuff isn't perfect prose. I considered tidying it up, but once you start messing around with a thing there's never any end to it, so I've left it pretty much as it is.

The transcripts are published in the order they were originally recorded, and are prefaced by the introduction to the *Anthology* DVD released by the Richard Dawkins Foundation for Reason and Science in April 2008 (the only video that hasn't appeared on the internet) in which I try to explain what I'm about. I hope it will serve as a mini introduction to this book as well.

0

Introduction to *Anthology* DVD

Released by the Richard Dawkins Foundation, April 2008

Hi everyone. I'm Pat Condell. Welcome to this video compilation.

If you've seen me on the internet then you probably know that I really don't care whether God created man or man created God, but I think whichever one was responsible deserves a really good kicking.

People often ask me why I feel the need to be abrasive, even insulting about religion. Well, I don't think I am insulting, quite honestly. I think I'm positively emollient, all things considered. But if on occasion I am insulting it's because that's the only way I can give religion the respect I think it deserves.

And, although I've got no special desire to offend anyone, let's be honest, if you're talking about religion and you're not offending people, then you're not really talking about religion, which I believe has shown itself to be completely unworthy as a conduit to higher understanding because it makes no attempt to understand anything. It already has all the answers, and not a single one supported by evidence.

Indeed, virtually every statement religion makes about reality is an open invitation to mockery and ridicule, so if I were to give it any respect at all I'm afraid I would instantly lose all respect for myself, because I believe that to be righteously certain about something you can't possibly know is the mark of a fool, and calling it faith doesn't give it any more dignity.

We also know that faith is often a get-out-of-jail card for crazy, so when faith is around crazy is never going to be too far away, which is not exactly a comforting thought in this looming age of nuclear theocracies.

Also, religion empowers mediocrity. It gives every inadequate control freak the authority to point God's wrathful finger and to unload the poison inside their own miserable heart on to some other poor bastard who's doing nothing wrong, but is doing something different.

It tells me that, as a human being, I must atone for the sin of existing. Well, I've tried, but I can't find anything wrong with existing. Maybe I've got a warped sense of values, but I just can't bring myself to see it as a crime. Sorry.

Of course I realise that there are people who get joy and fulfilment from their religious beliefs, and I've got no problem with any of that. Why should I have? What am I, a philistine? Of course not. Anyone who gets a good healthy buzz from their faith, good luck to them I say. It's the unhealthy buzz I have a problem with – the one that comes from the glorification of ignorance, from the indoctrination of children, and from the celebration of death. The one that wants to impose itself like a blanket of fog over everyone whether they like it or not.

And, as we encourage this mentality (which we do now constantly) to be more and more demanding and intrusive, and as every concession we make to it is, I believe, a step into darkness, I think this bubble of insanity needs to be burst, and not massaged.

So I'm not really here to be polite or to seek consensus. I'm not saying: "How can we work together to find a common understanding?" What I'm saying is something more along the lines of: "Get your insane beliefs out of my life, you ignorant manipulative liberty-taking sons of bitches." Something more like that. Just so you know what you're getting into here.

I'd like to thank the Richard Dawkins Foundation for their help with this project. If the video quality is not all it could be I'm afraid that's my fault, not theirs. When I started making these things I had no idea they would become in any way popular, so I didn't keep the originals. I hope you'll be able to forgive me for that, but, if not, fortunately I forgive myself.

Thank you for watching. I hope you enjoy the videos whether you agree with them or not.

I wish you peace, of course, but even more than that, may your children be atheists, for all our sakes.

1

Response to the Blasphemy Challenge

February 8, 2007

Hello everybody, I'm Pat Condell, and I deny the holy spirit. Yes, I do.

I deny the holy spirit in the morning, in the evening, and again last thing at night I make a point of actively denying the holy spirit.

Indeed, when I'm not busy denying the holy spirit I'm not doing anything, because guess what – I'm always denying the holy spirit.

That's right, waiting at a bus stop, you might be filing your nails or reading a magazine. I'm denying the holy spirit.

Walking down the street, you're gazing into shop windows, whereas I'm doing something useful – denying the holy spirit.

Why do I deny the holy spirit? Well, because if blasphemy was good enough for Jesus Christ, it's good enough for me.

And besides, like everyone else, I've seen what passes for the holy spirit in action, and I know that the holy spirit, if it ever existed, was long ago hijacked by criminals and liars, and is now as empty as a born again Christian smile.

And this is why denying the holy spirit now takes up so much of my time I'm literally burning the Bible at both ends.

That's right, whether awake or asleep, I joyously deny the holy spirit every day and in every way – upwards, downwards, backwards, forwards, sideways, inside out, back to front and upside down in perpetuity, or forever, whichever lasts longer.

Every moment of my life is a precious jewel of opportunity for me to deny the holy spirit and every nasty little thing it stands for.

Every breath I take, every word I utter, my every action down to the minutest detail is calculated specifically to deny the holy spirit – that spiteful, vindictive and truly unholy spirit of the mythical psychopath in the sky.

As for you, I can't tell you what to do. But if you've got any sense, and if you care about your children's sanity, you'll deny the holy spirit, because the holy spirit denies you, as it denies me, and all of humanity.

The holy spirit can be summed up in three words: "Thou shalt not!"

Whatever you want to do, you can't, you shouldn't, you mustn't, you won't. And if you do, you'll be tortured forever.

That's why the holy spirit is our enemy, not our friend. It wants us to deny our own nature, to remain fearful, ignorant and ashamed, to hate others as we hate ourselves, and to die without living, not to live without dying. And that in a nutshell is why I deny the holy spirit. Thank you very much. Peace.

2

Hello America

February 18, 2007

Hello America. I'm Pat Condell, and I'm your friend, because I live in the UK, and our two countries have quite a lot in common, apart from the fact that everyone else on the planet hates our guts.

We speak the same language, you and I, we share the same culture, more or less, and we worship the same god – a just god, a jealous god, a psychotic god whose vengeance is terrible to behold, especially if we've got anything to do with it. Praise the Lord.

Your president is a born again Christian, in the sense that Dracula was born again when he rose from the grave – or was that Jesus? Hmm. Do we drink his blood, or does he drink ours? I've often wondered about that one.

Our prime minister is also a Christian, although I'm not sure if he's been born again. Truth is a lot of people in my country are now sorry he was ever born in the first place.

But you have a particular brand of Christianity in America

which is unique and extremely creative, in that it bears absolutely no resemblance to the message of the prophet it supposedly reveres, and is in fact diametrically opposed to every single thing that he ever said without exception, which, if nothing else America, shows incredible balls on your part.

In Britain we have an established church, which means that we are officially a Christian country. But, like you, we don't discriminate. We'll sell arms to anyone, and we really don't care what atrocities they're used for, as long as the money is right, because business is business. Praise the Lord.

Because God is on our side we both know that when our country is doing evil it's good evil as opposed to evil evil. And we know that good evil always defeats evil evil, except when evil evil cunningly disguises itself as good evil and becomes born again – then you've got a whole new ballgame.

And your president plays this particular game very well indeed. We all know his history. We know how he used to be just a useless cocaine-snorting drink-driving draft-dodging daddy's little rich boy hellraiser, until one day, after a chat with Billy Graham, he had a revelation that he had been chosen by God to be a dangerous delusional bigot. He was quickly shoehorned into the governorship of Texas where he finally found he had a talent for something – signing death warrants, praise the Lord. And from there it was just a short step to George W. the Lionheart, president of all Christendom.

They say he's very well connected, your president, and this doesn't mean that his joints are all reinforced with steel wire – nothing as sinister as that. It simply means that he has a lot of corrupt and powerful friends who will stop at nothing to get their way. And by his own admission he invaded Iraq because one of these friends, namely God, instructed him to.

Now I'm not going to try and tell you that your president George W. Bush is insane, because the way I see it you don't actually need to be insane if you're George W. Bush. If you're a cynical small-minded nasty little born again hypocrite with a Bible in your hand, then frankly you're already holding a royal flush, and you don't need any more cards.

And besides, he's more than ably assisted in all his endeavours by our own insane Christian prime minister, another little man with blood on his hands which he didn't get from having nails hammered through them, although I'm sure his press office would like us to believe otherwise.

And we all know that he joined in with the invasion of Iraq because he felt the hand of history on his genitals, and because he wants a cowboy hat. The way he walks when he's with Bush, it's like they're on their way to the OK Corral, or some other gay club.

But it turns out that some people in Iraq, for some inexplicable reason, don't actually want freedom and democracy imposed on them from outside, which just proves the truth in the old saying, America, that you can lead a horse to water, but you can't make him suck your cock.

But never mind, because we're still here, and we still love you. Yes, we do. And let me just say that we don't feel at all used or defiled by you, America. Well, maybe we do just a little. Actually, maybe quite a lot. But it's worth it for the privilege of being friends with you, even if you do insist on taking our fingerprints before you'll let us into your country.

Because frankly, America, you've saved our bacon. If not for you, we wouldn't be the high profile country we are in the world today. Having lost an empire we were ready to be shunted away into the sidelines of history and forgotten.

But now, thanks to you and your glorious mission from God, we find that we still have a role to play in the world, poking our nose in where it's not wanted, stealing and wasting every precious resource we can get our greedy hands on, and kicking the shit out of brown people – the way Jesus would have wanted.

So thank you for that, America. I can't tell you how proud that makes me feel. I really, really can't. But it's human nature to live in hope, so let me just say in closing, America, as one friend to another, get well real soon. We're all praying for you. Peace.

3

What Have I Got Against Religion?

March 4, 2007

Somebody asked me this week: "What have you got against religion?"

That's a tough one. I'm suspicious of religion, and that's unusual for me because normally if something sounds too good to be true, I'm in – where do I sign?

But with religion, something is holding me back, and I'm not sure what it is. It could be the shameless hypocrisy, the arrogant self-righteousness, the wilful ignorance, or the cynical indoctrination and poisoning of young minds with prejudice and hate. It's difficult to say exactly.

I do know that, given half a chance, religion would control every aspect of my life whether I want it to or not, and would impose a morality on me, telling me what to think, what to believe, and who to attack and kill for believing something else.

Thus, religion is the natural home of the psychopath.

Historically, whenever religion gets any power the result is always repression.

If it could, I'm sure it would bring back crucifixion. So that's one thing I've got against religion.

Another thing, since you ask, is this book *(holds up Bible)*, the Bible, or the Holy Bible, as it's jokingly referred to here on the front cover; the costume drama from hell, a mesmerising soup' of image and metaphor into which any fantasy can be read, and by which any horror can be justified.

They call the Bible the good book, and yes, if you're looking for blood and guts, sadistic cruelty, meanness of spirit, and general psychopathic insanity, then this might be what you'd call a good book – this might be the book for you.

But if you're looking in the Bible for a guide to living a compassionate, wise and humane life, well then frankly you've got more chance of finding a lap dancing club in Mecca, or a virgin in a Catholic orphanage.

If this book is truly the word of a loving and merciful God, then all I can say is it's a suicide note.

Although, I will admit it's possible for the Bible to be used for good, of course it is. For example, if you were to take a nice thick hardback copy of the Bible, insert it sideways into George W. Bush's born again anus, and then hammer it up there nice and tight with a very large mallet, that might do some good.

I'm no expert, but I really think it would do him good, and I also think it would greatly enhance America's somewhat tarnished image abroad. You know it makes sense.

Finally, to all the Christians who have contacted me recently, quoting scripture and preaching Jesus – you know who you are. Yes please, by all means carry on preaching Jesus to me all you like, that's fine. But if you're not also imitating Jesus in your daily life then you might want to think about preaching something that's more in line with your actual beliefs, and not your pretend ones, otherwise you could go a little crazy.

In other words, if you can't practise what you preach, then at least have the decency to preach what you practise.

Well, those are just a few of the things I've got against religion. If anyone has any more stupid questions I'll be happy to answer them as well. Peace.

4

The Trouble with Islam

March 16, 2007

I'd like to say a few things about Islam, if I may.

Here in the UK religion was always pretty dormant until Muslims came along and started burning books, passing death sentences, and generally demanding special treatment for no good reason.

But they showed everyone else what can be achieved by bullying and intimidation, so now every crackpot in the country feels entitled to respect for their precious beliefs – beliefs often lifted wholesale from the ramblings of some ancient desert nomad with a psychological disorder.

It does seem quite ironic to me that the very people who have clearly made no attempt to think for themselves are always the most vocal in demanding respect for their "ideas".

Some Muslims go further and claim they're victimised in British society, but I don't believe that's true. I do think people are getting fed up with hearing about Muslims all the time, and they wish Muslims would just shut up and get on with their lives instead of constantly bellyaching about nothing. But that's not the same as being victimised.

But, because we live in a liberal democracy, and therefore have certain double standards to maintain, any criticism of Islam or of Muslims draws the immediate accusation of Islamophobia, a dishonest word which seeks to portray legitimate comment as some kind of hate crime, when the truth is Islam has a chip on its shoulder the size of a mosque and it looks to take offence at every opportunity.

Some Muslims, it seems, are almost permanently offended about something or other. And yet you never hear a peep out of any of these people when some young Muslim girl is murdered for bringing dishonour upon her insane family. Suddenly everyone's looking at the floor then.

They keep telling us that Islam is a religion of peace, but all the evidence says it's a religion of war. Its holy book urges Muslims to conquer the world and subjugate everyone to the rule of God.

If Islam had its way elections would become a thing of the past, and the rest of us would be living in the past for the foreseeable future.

And some people are very keen to bring this situation about, especially these loud-mouthed rabble-rousing Islamic clerics who we always hear praising the suicide bombers as glorious martyrs. Yet curiously you never hear about any of these enthusiasts blowing themselves up for the glory of God. They're always very keen to delegate that particular honour. Despite the guarantee of all those luscious virgins waiting for them in heaven, these guys are so selfless that they can always find somebody more deserving.

Of course, the whole seventy-two virgins scenario has become something of a comedy staple, and with good reason, but it does have one serious problem, and that is that the virgins are likely to be good wholesome Islamic virgins (because there won't be any infidel riffraff in heaven) so presumably they'll have brothers and cousins and uncles who are all determined to defend their honour by killing anyone who makes eye contact with them. They haven't really thought this whole thing through, it seems to me. For this they blow themselves up? Wouldn't it be easier just to get an inflatable woman and blow her up? And then if one of your friends happens to glance at her with lustful eyes, you can simply stone her to death and get another one in the usual way.

Also, I think Muslim women in Britain who cover their faces are mentally ill. I realise that in some parts of the world women don't actually have any choice in this matter, governed as they are by primitive pigs whose only achievement in life is to be born with a penis in one hand and a Koran in the other. But it just seems to me that if God had intended you to cover your face then in his wisdom he would have provided you with a flap of skin for the purpose. Of course if it gave you any sexual pleasure it would have to be removed; that goes without saying.

But I don't want to be too hard on Islam here for two reasons. Firstly, I don't want to be murdered by some hysterical self-righteous carpet-chewing book-burning muppet with shit for brains.

And secondly, I think we do need to make allowances for Islam, because we have to remember that it is quite a young religion, so maybe right now it's just going through a difficult age; a little headstrong, full of itself, thinks it knows all the answers – but I'm sure it will learn.

I think years from now a lot of intelligent Muslims will be looking back all this medievalism and jihad nonsense with embarrassment and shame, like the Germans do with the Nazis, and maybe then we can all have a good laugh about it.

But in the meantime, I think any religion that demands earthly vengeance and retribution, for any reason, is not really a religion at all, but an illness, and should be treated as such.

Peace, and I mean that most sincerely.

5

What Do I Believe?

March 28, 2007

I've just had an e-mail from a Christian who says: "You're very quick to mock other people's beliefs, but what do you believe?"

It's a fair question. I believe that if God exists he's either insane or dead.

I believe that if you've got nothing but scripture between your ears, then you've got nothing between your ears.

I believe that if the Bible is the word of God, and if the Koran is the word of God, then God must have two words, and I believe I can guess what they are as well.

But then I believe you won't find the truth in any book; you have to look within.

(I don't know where that came from; I must have read it somewhere.)

I believe that the Holy Land is the most inappropriate place name in human history, with the possible exception of Sunderland's Stadium of Light.

And I believe that Jesus Christ, if he ever existed, is dead, and he's going to stay dead just like everybody else.

But if by some miracle he did come back, I believe he'd be embarrassed to be worshipped, ashamed of Christianity, and disgusted by Christians. Because I believe that telling someone they'll burn forever in hell is a form of psychological assault which should be outlawed like any other nasty little hate crime.

I believe the Christian Church itself in particular is an evil carbuncle on the soul of humanity which is actively engaged in carrying out the express work of Satan.

And if you're offended by this then that's too bad, because I also believe that nobody has the right not to be offended, and anyone who thinks they do *(holds up middle finger)* can sit on this and swivel.

I believe there's more spirituality in a single flower than in all the sanctimonious sky pilots who have ever lived. And that's why I believe there should be a link between Church and state – all clergy should go to prison for fraud.

I believe that the only heaven you'll ever know is right here on earth. And if you can't see that, you are not really looking.

I believe that faith-based education is a social cancer which serves only to produce new generations of ignorant bigots, and I believe that indoctrinating children with this repressive medieval bullshit should be vigorously prosecuted as child abuse.

I believe that religious belief itself is a form of mental illness which has outstayed its welcome on this planet and should now be relegated back to the realm of tarot cards and crystal balls where it belongs.

If you have to worship something try worshipping something real, like the planet that gave you life, because it's the best friend you ever had. And I believe it's the only friend you will ever have. Peace.

6

Happy Easter

April 5, 2007

Happy Easter, everyone. Yes, it's that time of year again when we celebrate one of the oldest Christian traditions, the blood sacrifice.

Just as two thousand years ago God sent his son to die for our sins because he didn't have the balls to do it himself, so Bush and Blair now send other people's sons to die for their sins for much the same reason.

But this is not really a time for politics, is it? This is a very special week, as we know, because this week it's all about the Easter bunny being nailed to a hot cross bun so that he can come back and redeem mankind at some point in the future.

It's often said that Jesus could have saved himself, but he chose not to. And if you read the Gospels it's clear he could have talked himself out of that crucifixion quite easily, but he was just too stubborn. The Romans didn't really want to kill him at all, but in the end they went along with it because he was being such a prick about it.

The truth is he couldn't wait to get up on that cross. In fact I think Christianity only exists because Jesus Christ just happened to be a masochist. I think he took one look at the hammer and nails and he couldn't believe his luck. He thought: "In three days I'll be in heaven, but until then I'm going to enjoy myself."

Now this, of course, is just a theory, I want to emphasise that, because nobody knows what really happened. The Gospels are not eye-witness accounts. The evangelists never made it to the crucifixion. Couldn't get tickets, I guess. Once they knew Mel Gibson was coming I'm sure everybody wanted to be there.

And, to be fair to him, he has made what is now probably the definitive movie on the Easter story – *The Passion of the Christ*, which, when it first came out, was subjected to quite a lot of criticism and abuse, mainly because it's a cynical piece of gratuitous trash aimed at simple-minded born again plankton.

For this reason, though, it made a lot of money, so now some Hollywood studios get a panel of Christians to vet their movies before release to ensure they won't offend any ignorant born again shitkickers who might happen to be watching. The future looks bright for American culture, wouldn't you say? I wonder if years from now we'll look back and say: Poor America, it could have saved itself, but it chose not to?

As for Jesus himself, well, every day for the last two thousand years he's been on the verge of coming back to redeem us all, but he hasn't actually shown up yet, and to be perfectly honest with you I'm not a bit surprised. Put yourself in his position. Would you come back if you were him? I wouldn't, but then I wouldn't have come in the first place, so I might be the wrong person to ask.

The only thing that bothers me about all this is that when Jesus does arrive to dispense his particular brand of justice he's only going to save the people who believe in him, and the rest of us, the non-believers, will be consigned to the eternal flames of hellfire.

But where's the justice there? Whatever happened to: "Do unto others as you would be done by" – or is that all being quietly forgotten now?

And how ironic, too, that I am now being victimised as a non-believer. I'm being persecuted for my beliefs, by Jesus Christ, the one person who you really would expect to know better. He could save me but he's choosing not to. What a Judas.

Still, on the other hand nobody's perfect, so I'll forgive him. Why not? I'm in a good mood. It's Easter. Peace.

7

Absolute Certainty

April 13, 2007

Although I'm an atheist, I prefer to think of myself as an agnostic fundamentalist. In other words I don't know, I don't think anyone else knows either, and anyone who disagrees with me is a filthy infidel swine. I'm sorry about that last bit, but apparently those are the rules.

Of course it's fun to speculate, and it's been human nature ever since the first caveman watched an eagle soaring above the clouds and thought to himself: "I wonder what that tastes like. Might be nice with potatoes and gravy."

We've always speculated about what might lie beyond the stars, an activity a bit like theology, only without all the cast iron certainties.

And it's fun to speculate about the big questions like the meaning of life, because you never know, somebody might actually come up with the answer. So far nobody has, which would explain why there are so many expert opinions on the subject.

But there's just something about human beings when it comes to the unknown, that we don't seem able to just wonder about something and speculate creatively, maybe have a bit of fun with it. No, not us. Instead we like to decide beyond all possible doubt without a single shred of evidence. We prefer to nail our colours to the mast before we even know if there's a ship attached to it, and often we'll defend that position to the death. If that doesn't qualify as serious mental illness I would love to be briefed on what exactly does qualify, and why.

It's unfortunate that many people on this planet seem to believe the very first thing they're told, and stick with it for the rest of their life.

Not only does it remain unexamined, but any attempt to challenge it is taken as a grievous insult.

Clearly those early few months and years of life are a very sensitive time, and whatever ideas are imprinted into the soft putty of the unformed mind at that stage stay there pretty much forever.

And yet for some reason here in the civilised world it's still perfectly legal for us to indoctrinate our children with the most hateful and divisive absurdities it would be possible to imagine (and imagine them we have), creating in them not young vibrant healthy inquiring minds, but rather stunted little freakish bonsai minds that are no use to anyone but a bloodsucking preacher.

We not only allow this abuse, we actively encourage it. We throw public money at it when we'd be better off subsidising the tobacco industry, because that does less harm. At least cigarettes carry a health warning. How about a mental health warning on the holy scriptures?

Especially now that, for the first time since the middle ages, faith and politics go together like sex and violence, only this time space-age weapons are controlled by stone-age minds, and right now, especially in the Middle East, things are shaping up quite nicely to blow us all to kingdom come. Except that no kingdom is going to come, because this is the kingdom. It has already come, and we're already living the dream.

Religion knows this, but it doesn't want us to know it, because then it would no longer have any reason to exist. So instead it seeks to place itself, to position itself, between us and our experience. A self-appointed filter. A parasite.

Now maybe that's OK with you. Maybe you're fine with that because maybe you don't want experience. Maybe you prefer dreams. Maybe you want your head to go to that special place where God wreaks vengeance on anyone whose lifestyle you don't personally happen to approve of, and where Jesus strokes you like a puppy dog. Well, if that's the case then you might as well take drugs, because you're already on the most dangerous drug there is.

Absolute certainty is a drug that can make people do the strangest things. It's the devil's drug, and you don't want to be around anyone who's on that stuff, because they're no longer in control. You can see it in their eyes, the drug is controlling them, so that suddenly no action is too callous or too spiteful or too cruel to be justified.

And if you get hooked on it, and if you keep taking it, you too could wake up one day so full of righteousness that suddenly the only thing that makes sense to you any more is somebody else's death.

And you'll realise that your mind is no longer your best friend.

So if somebody offers you absolute certainty, they're going to make it sound attractive, and you will be tempted, but just say no. Your mind, and your children's minds, will thank you for it, and that really is an absolute certainty. Peace.

8

Religion in the UK

April 17, 2007

Hi everyone. I've been asked by ptolemi* to say a few words about religion here in Britain.

Well, as you probably know, we're a Christian country like you are in America. We're not quite as Christian as you are because, after all, you've still got the death penalty, but traditionally we practise a form of Christianity almost as psychopathically disengaged from the message of Christ as you do, although nowadays we're more of a multifaith society. And what that means in practice is that everybody wants respect but nobody wants to give any, so we all get offended at the drop of a hat, or a turban – it doesn't make much difference. Christians, Muslims, Sikhs, Jews. Everybody, it seems, has some sort of beef (except the Hindus, obviously).

Everybody complains in Britain that religion doesn't get

* YouTube user.

enough respect, and yet there are sixteen churches within a ten minute walk of my house, not to mention mosques and temples and synagogues and all the other assorted wendy houses of the soul that cover this land from top to bottom like a plague of boils. And yet religion doesn't get enough respect?

It pays no tax on corporate profits, it's allowed to indoctrinate children from birth, yet it doesn't get enough respect?

Well, excuse me, but even the royal family doesn't get quite that much respect, and they're treated like royalty.

A third of all the schools in Britain are single faith schools, financially supported by the government.

Teachers are against this. In fact, just this week teachers demanded a ban on all faith schools because they encourage segregation and prejudice, so naturally the government is creating even more of them, because our prime minister is a well-known Christian hypocrite who has publicly endorsed the teaching of creationism in schools.

Meanwhile, schools are dropping the Holocaust from history lessons, in case Muslim children who have been taught to hate Jews feel compelled to say something anti-Semitic. We don't want to embarrass the Muslim kids by showing up their parents as hate-mongering bigots, because that would be disrespectful to their faith.

I'm just wondering how long before we start referring to it as the Holocaust theory, for the sake of community relations.

Christians, meanwhile, are becoming a lot more vocal here in Britain because they're worried about the growth of Islam. They don't want to see the country swamped by a new foreign religion.

They'd rather keep the old foreign religion, the one that stole the pagans' festivals and burned them all as witches in the name of Jesus the merciful.

The Church of England is doing its best to keep the flame alive, so to speak. The Church is very much part of the establishment here in Britain. We even let some of its bishops sit in Parliament and help decide our laws, which explains why we're still not allowed to go shopping on Easter Sunday.

The Church of England was originally established about five hundred years ago primarily to allow King Henry VIII to abandon and murder his wives with God's blessing, but now that purpose has been served it's become something of a joke organisation which is often referred to as the Conservative Party in drag.

Right now the leaders of the Church are preoccupied, not with homelessness or poverty or injustice, but whether it's right for one man to insert his penis into another man's anus in private. This is what they're focussed on, and we all know that you get what you focus on, which is probably why half of them joined the Church in the first place.

One person I do feel a little sorry for, though, is the Archbishop of Canterbury – the most important clergyman in Britain, and he's only got two lousy palaces to live in. What sort of life is that for a man of God? I bet if Jesus came back even he'd be embarrassed for him. I bet he wouldn't be able to look him in the eye.

But anyway that's pretty much how things stand here in Britain. Religion is alive and well, in the sense that a crocodile that's swimming towards you is alive and well, and its influence is growing as steadily as a clergyman's penis in a roomful of choirboys.

But here now, as in America, people are starting to speak out against this creeping insanity, and who knows, if enough of us do it maybe one day humanity will come to its senses and we can finally put this fake God into a rocket ship and send the silly old fool back into thin air where he came from. I'm looking forward to it. Peace.

9

In Jesus' Name

April 25, 2007

You want to know what I think? I think Satan has been born again. I really do. I think he has accepted Jesus into his heart because he knows a good racket when he sees one.

Here in the UK we've now got an evangelical television channel. It's the kind of thing that will be very familiar to everyone in the United States, especially if you've ever switched on your TV set on a Sunday morning and seen one holy man after another urging you to send money so that Jesus can buy a new Cadillac. Apparently, Jesus can't save the world until he's been properly kitted out with a million dollar mansion and a private jet. Some small print in the Gospels that we must have missed.

They spend a lot of their time praising the lord and praying, these people (when they're not having extramarital sex with rentboys, obviously), and preaching about a heaven that sounds to me like the afterlife from hell, because they're all going to be there.

And everything they do, they do in Jesus' name. This is one thing I've noticed, that almost every second sentence is followed by the words: "In Jesus' name."

Every fake healing and every insincere blessing, every lowdown skulking mean-spirited nasty mealy-mouthed double-talking lie they tell, is told in Jesus' name.

Like baking soda, Jesus' name just helps to take away some of the unpleasant odour of what they're really all about, which is raking in mountains of cold hard cash, all tax free, so ultimately paid for by you and me. In Jesus' name, of course.

In a way you can't really blame the televangelists, because they're only behaving according to their nature as blood-sucking predators. And they do fulfil a need, of sorts, because it's said that about a third of the population are what's called true believers, people who want to believe, who have a need to believe, and who are determined to believe in something. So you don't even have to threaten these people with damnation. They already want to believe your bullshit, and more importantly they want to give you their money, like chickens throwing themselves into the fox's mouth. What self-respecting conman is going to turn down that opportunity, any more than the fox is going to say: "No chicken for me thank you, I'll just have a salad."

And they've got such a good sales pitch, too. It's just irresistible. "If you send us money, you're preaching the Gospel. And the more money you send, the more Gospel you'll be preaching."

What a dilemma. What should I do with my last few dollars, should I feed the kids today, or should I do something useful with it and preach a little more Gospel, in Jesus' name?

In some ways you've just got to hold your hands up in admiration at the sheer barefaced effrontery of the whole operation. But the problem is they use this vast wealth to buy influence in government and to interfere in other people's lives. And personally, that's where I draw the line.

So, if you'd like to have some fun, and I suspect that you would, I had an e-mail from the people at a website called earthsgreatestlawsuit.org,* and they tell me they intend to sue organised corporate religion right back into the slimy hole it crawled from for making advertising claims that it can't justify and for selling a product that it can't deliver, which is of course illegal. And, if you'd like to, you can help them do it, and it won't cost you a penny. Doesn't that sound like fun?

And the best thing is, if you've read the Sermon on the Mount, you'll know it's what he would have wanted, so you really can do it in Jesus' name. What a wonderful blessing for us all. Peace.

* The website no longer exists, alas.

10

United States of Jesus

May 3, 2007

Hi everyone. I've had quite a lot of e-mails and comments about my videos so far, mostly very positive and supportive, so thank you to everybody for that.

Predictably some people have been less than friendly. Some have told me they hope I die a horrible death. I've been threatened with all kinds of violent retribution, and I've been called some pretty inventively disgusting names because of course the human imagination is very fertile, as we know from reading the scriptures.

One guy was particularly preoccupied with anuses and boners for some reason. I think he had a thing for Jesus.

But some people even went so far as to call me anti-American, which has got to be the stupidest thing I've ever heard. Actually, I take that back. Intelligent design is the stupidest thing I've ever heard, but that one runs it pretty close.

No, I'm not anti-American. What I am is anti-stupidity, anti-ignorance and anti-bigotry, and I suppose that could be construed as anti-American if you're a stupid ignorant bigot, but I think most intelligent people would see it as very pro-American.

I do think it's a shame that America, like Britain, is governed by criminals. But there's not much we can do about that because we live in a democracy.

What are you going to do? Vote? Yeah right. Good luck with that.

No, I'm much more concerned about America's relationship with God, because that's not actually based on anything real, whereas its consequences are extremely real for everybody on the planet, including me.

So excuse me if I'm a little picky about this, but I just don't think that anyone who's looking forward to the afterlife is qualified to run any country, and right now in the United States of Jesus it's easier for a camel to pass through the eye of a needle than it is for an atheist to be elected president.

The American people have made it clear they want a born again Christian president, even if it meant putting a ten gallon hat on a half pint head, because in the land of the free in the twenty-first century if you don't believe that Jesus Christ rose from the dead and physically ascended into heaven, and that we're all going to join him there just as soon as we can arrange the end of the world, then, my friend, you are not fit for public office.

And this is why there's now daily Bible study in the White House and in the Pentagon, because they're all experts on their Bible in those two places. They know all about who begat whom, and who smote whom, and who spake unto whom, but they're not quite sure where Italy is.

But maybe I'm wrong to be concerned about all this, or about the fact that forty-five percent of Republican voters call themselves born again evangelical Christians (and they don't mean it as an insult). Or that President Bush senior says he doesn't think atheists should even be considered citizens. Or that so many people in the world's most advanced country don't want evolution taught in schools because they believe the earth was formed six thousand years ago, shortly after the invention of the wheel. It was a world where people and dinosaurs lived together, apparently, just like in the Flintstones.

And this is appropriate, because to me America is like a dinosaur, a massive powerful animal with a tiny brain.

My country, Britain, is like a much smaller animal, but with a brain that's just as tiny; those two things could rattle around together like two peas in a bucket, and you couldn't tell them apart.

So if I'm anti-American, I'm also anti-British, because I'm anti-stupid.

And yes, that would include anyone who thinks America is one nation under God any more than it was before the Pledge of Allegiance was hijacked by Christian zealots.

Or that "In God we trust" is some kind of American national motto any more than it was before the currency was hijacked by Christian zealots.

The truth is America is not a nation under God at all. It's a nation under a spell. It's only a matter of time before these people start pushing for the cross to be shown on the American flag. You think I'm joking, but you know I'm not.

Now the real irony here, of course, is that if Jesus Christ was American president what a different world this would be. But of course that's just an impossible dream, because there's no way that Jesus would ever be elected president. How many right-wing Christians are going to vote for a liberal Jew? You've got more chance of getting blood out of a Jehovah's Witness. He's from the Middle East and he looks like a goddamned hippie. The Fox network would crucify him, if he hadn't already been arrested as a terrorist.

No, I think right now America is just a little too Christian for Jesus.

But I'm optimistic that this will change, because I love America and everything it stands for. Well, everything it originally stood for before it was hijacked by Christian zealots.

And I know that if everybody on the planet followed the principles of the American Constitution this would be a much more civilised world than it is.

Right now it's a world of chaos, choking under the poison cloud of religious dogma. Wherever you look, from the Indian subcontinent to the Middle East to Africa to the future Islamic republic of Europe, you know in your heart that if America isn't going to lead us out of the Dark Ages, nobody is.

And that's why you won't find anybody on this planet who is more pro-American than I am.

Thank you very much, and peace, especially to Americans.

11

Why Are We Friends with Saudi Arabia?

May 14, 2007

Despite the current war on terror, or Islam, or whatever you want to call it, both Britain and America are still very good friends with certain Arab countries because these countries provide us with a valuable service. They allow us to send people we don't like to their countries to be tortured legally, and that way we're not doing anything morally wrong.

One of these countries is the kingdom of Saudi Arabia, which is well known as an exclusively Islamic country. None of this multifaith nonsense for them. In fact, it's against the law even to preach Christianity in Saudi Arabia, and the penalty is death. Well, that would certainly put a stop to it, so let's not dismiss it out of hand.

This is because they subscribe to sharia law, the Islamic legal code, which has been designed to put the fear of God into men and to put the fear of men into women, it seems to me –

particularly the fear of men with beards into women.

But there's an irony here, because everybody knows that Muslims don't drink alcohol; they won't have a drink, not even at Christmas. And yet sharia law has a lot in common with The Campaign for Real Ale. Both were devised by men with beards for the benefit of men with beards.

The big difference, of course, is The Campaign for Real Ale doesn't have women stoned to death for no reason. And a very good thing too. After all, somebody's got to work the bar, and then somebody's got to drive afterwards. Well done, lads. That's using the brain. Congratulations on that one.

Now despite the fact that most of the 9/11 lunatics were Saudis, and a quite a few prominent Saudis were spirited out of the United States by the Bush family before the FBI could ask them why they did it, we're still friends with Saudi Arabia because they've got lots and lots of oil. In fact it would be difficult to think of a more oily country than Saudi Arabia.

You might say: Why be friends with people like this? They're obviously scumbags. Why don't we just go in there and take the oil like we usually do?

But if we did that they wouldn't buy any more weapons from us, and our whole economy would probably collapse.

And this is why, for example, the Saudis were able to embarrass the British government recently (and with their record that takes some doing) by threatening to cancel a massive arms deal if the British police continued to investigate bribery allegations against members of their so-called royal family. Naturally, our government caved in to these threats like a paper cup because apparently it's in our country's interests to brown-nose a bunch of sleazy medieval gangsters, which in my opinion makes us almost as creepy as the Bush family, and I thought that was genuinely impossible.

Now I'm not saying there's anything wrong with Saudi Arabia that couldn't be cured by civilisation, because it's not my place to say that. The truth is I haven't visited the country, so, for example, I've never had the privilege of attending a public execution. Watching somebody have their head removed with a sword, what's uncivilised about that, apart from the fact that you can't get a cold beer to enjoy while you're watching it? Now that really is uncivilised.

No, I've never been to Saudi Arabia, so I've never had the chance to witness the religious police prevent the rescue of young women from a burning building because they're not wearing the correct headgear. I wasn't actually there when those fifteen young girls burned to death for absolutely no reason, so I can't comment on it, and I wouldn't dream of doing so. That would be disrespectful.

And anyway, just because Saudi Arabia is single-handedly responsible for the poisonous Wahhabi brand of fundamentalist Islam that has plagued this planet like the AIDS virus for the last few decades, and just because Saudi Arabia finances the murderous madrassas in Pakistan where the London bombers learned their godless ideology, that doesn't mean I've got anything against the place or its rulers. Far from it – about that far from it. *(Shows finger and thumb very slightly apart.)*

But if I could just make one small positive suggestion.

Everybody knows that Saudi Arabia is very rich in certain mineral deposits – notably, of course, sand. My goodness me, it's got so much sand it could export the stuff. Or even better, it could import a load of water and cement, mix itself into a giant block of concrete and do us all a huge favour.

Oh, and another thing, nobody is going to convince me that the king of Saudi Arabia has never had a drink. I don't care what you say, with his money there's no way that he just limits himself to cocaine and hookers. He looks like a Jack Daniel's man to me. Obviously, I can't prove that statement, but then we all know you don't need proof when you've got faith.

Peace. You know it makes sense.

12

Am I a Racist?

May 20, 2007

Well, it seems that my little video about Islam has caused a storm in a teacup in Berkeley, California, where somebody on the grandly named Peace and Justice Commission circulated it in an e-mail, and everybody was shocked and disgusted. Well, they said they were shocked and disgusted, which is not really the same thing.

One person even called it hate speech, as if I'm some kind of neo-Nazi. Give me a break, I'm not even a Catholic any more.

Of course I don't want to offend Muslims. What do you think I am, insane? But I don't think that any intelligent Muslim would be offended by anything I've said. Indeed, I've had e-mails from Muslims who agree with me.

On the other hand, I don't really mind the idea of offending a group of politically correct jackasses, which is what seems to have happened in Berkeley.

If any of you dishonest wretches are watching this video, I

want to say to you that having an opinion about Muslim women covering their faces is not racist, and by calling it that you simply devalue that word even more than it's already been devalued by people like you.

I don't care what your race is, if you're walking around in public with your face covered up, dressed like a pepper pot, then I think you've got something wrong with you.

And it has nothing to do with religion or with God or anything like that. This is a social issue. This is a controlling device which has been imposed by men; ignorant cowardly men who are too insecure in themselves to allow women to be themselves.

It's a statement of segregation and of separation, and it's a wilful refusal to assimilate, and too often it's used cynically as a political weapon, to cause division in society.

They insist on working as teachers dressed in this costume, knowing it's going to cause problems because the kids can't hear what they're saying, and so it all ends up in court, because that's what they really wanted all along, and then it's all over the news again, because some Muslims have gone out of their way to be offended yet again.

I think that for any woman in a free country like Britain or America to deliberately wear this symbol of oppression, which is what it is, is an insult to all the brave women in Muslim countries who have already died horrible deaths trying to shake off this ridiculous medieval nonsense. I think they ought to be ashamed of themselves. And if you think that's racist, then I think you're the one who has the problem, not me.

I live in Britain, and we're a very tolerant society. Some people say we're too tolerant for our own good, but I'm proud of how tolerant we are. And that's why we tolerate people calling us racists, while simultaneously calling us kuffars and devils. We tolerate people teaching their children to hate Jews. We tolerate people using free speech to protest against free speech. We even tolerate people who despise the values that make this country the kind of place they'd want to come to, from whatever repressive hell hole they couldn't wait to get out of.

We couldn't be less racist if we tried, and we try all the time. Because we know that being tolerant means you have to tolerate intolerance, and you have to put up with people who don't want to put up with you. And that's what we do in Britain.

We bend over backwards for Muslims, all Muslims, almost as far as we bend over forwards for the American government, and that's all the way.

Peace.* And you can take that any way you like in Berkeley.

---

* I reverse the peace sign to make a V-sign, the British equivalent of giving the finger.

13

Miracles and Morals

May 29, 2007

Hi everyone. I've been asked by various people where I get my morality without religion. Well, isn't it obvious? I get it by mail order. That's right, it comes in a plain brown wrapper because I don't want the neighbours to know what I'm up to.

No, seriously, I simply ask myself, what would a Christian do in this situation? And then I do the opposite.

I'm kidding, of course. No, I just trust my feelings to tell me that good things are right and bad things are wrong, and it just seems to fall into place. I dunno, maybe it's a miracle.

Well, what's the alternative? A Christian morality that embraces all the barbarism of Leviticus while ignoring the simple wisdom in the golden rule? Thanks, but no thanks.

Even if you believe the Bible, you know that Adam and Eve gave us the knowledge of good and evil, which presumably means right and wrong. So why do we still need guidance? (If you can call it guidance, being bullied and threatened with violence by some celestial thug.)

I'm actually amazed that anyone even trusts God to tell us how to behave. If you used him as a role model you'd probably end up in prison, because that son of a bitch is about as qualified to preach morality as Charles Manson.

On every second page of the Old Testament somebody is being butchered for the glory of, or directly by, God. This is not a loving entity I see in these pages. This is a deeply disturbed individual. This is the kind of personality the police always tell you not to approach. This character would give Hitler a run for his money. And any morality that's there is really just a list of rules, some of them quite barbaric, which must be obeyed on pain of eternal torture (what else?).

But this is not really surprising, is it, because scripture is not actually about morality. It's really about believing in the impossible, and the more impossible a thing appears to be, the more likely we are to believe it, it seems to me.

And the morality is really just a garnish, a dressing, which is usually ignored for the meat and potatoes of the magic and the mumbo-jumbo.

For example, if you take the words of Jesus in the Sermon on the Mount, which is probably his greatest ever gig, and strip away all the Christianity, well then you'd have something worthwhile. But all the miracle stuff – the virgin birth, the resurrection, redemption, hellfire, damnation, and all the Cecil B. deMille stuff – that has all been put there deliberately to obscure this simple fact.

The last thing any clergyman wants is people living according to the words of Jesus, because if they did, there'd be no need for organised religion, and a lot of people would find themselves out of a job. They need the miracles to keep the cash rolling in, even though they tell us it's not actually about the miracles, it's about the message. Oh yeah? And what message would that be, then? "Believe in me, for behold, I can do miracles." That's the message, because if you take away the miracles what are you left with? A pretty decent guy talking common sense, which means that nobody on this planet is going to take him seriously if he lives to be a million. The miracles are everything. And all the stuff that Jesus said about blessed are the poor in spirit, the meek, the peacemakers; you're the salt of the earth, the light of the world, turn the other cheek, don't give alms in public, don't pray in public, you can't serve God and mammon, consider the lilies of the field, judge not lest ye be judged, don't be a hypocrite, whatever you ask for you'll get, do unto others as you want to be done by, beware of false prophets…

People have said that stuff for thousands of years, and nobody has ever listened.

So let's drop this idea that it's not about the miracles. It's all about the miracles. It's all about the magic and the mumbo-jumbo, which is a shame, because I think that's probably the last thing Jesus would have wanted. Of course, I can't be absolutely sure about that because, after all, I'm no theologian.

But given all this, I'd now like to ask you, where do you get your morality from? I'd be very interested to know. In the meantime, peace to everyone, especially Christians with guns who support the death penalty.

14

Catholic Morality

June 4, 2007

Well, not content with trying to force religion into the European constitution, now the Catholic Church is interfering in British politics. This week a cardinal and an archbishop have both threatened to withhold communion from Catholics MPs who don't vote against abortion.

Personally, I've always thought it's a shame the virgin Mary never had the right to choose, because then we might have been spared two thousand years of misery and bloodshed.

But it wasn't to be, and so, for Catholics, abortion has always been a tricky one, especially if you're using a knitting needle in a back alley, which is the Catholic Church's preferred method, because, when it comes to Catholic dogma, human life is only sacred if you obey the rules. Hence no condoms for Africa. We don't want those people doing anything immoral, so we're going to let them die.

This is from an organisation supposedly founded on the

teachings of Jesus. I'm not sure what teachings exactly. It must be the bit where Jesus talks about living in palaces full of art treasures, protecting paedophiles, and collaborating with the Nazis. I haven't actually managed to find that passage myself, but I'm sure it must be in the Gospels somewhere.

And this is why I wasn't too surprised when I first heard that the current Pope is in fact an ex-Nazi,* because to me the Catholic Church and Nazism go together as naturally as Bibles and lynch mobs. If you think of one, it's difficult not to think of the other.

Indeed, I've often thought it was just bad luck for the Catholic Church that Nazism never became respectable, because they put all their chips on the number of the beast, but it just didn't happen for them.

Although the Pope who collaborated with Hitler by ignoring the Holocaust is now being made a saint for his trouble. That's right, Pius XII is being made a saint, which has got to be the cheekiest thing I've heard since Henry Kissinger had the nerve to accept the Nobel Peace Prize.

I'm not sure why it is that the Catholic Church exudes this aura of, not so much evil as… well, actually yes, evil.

I think this whole celibacy thing has a lot to answer for, because there's got to be so much repressed energy there with nowhere to go. I mean that's bound to cause a few short circuits.

I can understand somebody being celibate if that's how they're comfortable. But if you're doing it as a penance, denying your

---

* OK, I know he was conscripted into it as a youth, so I admit that was a cheap shot, but I think this guy deserves a few cheap shots, so I'm not going to lose any sleep over it.

most powerful basic urges because you think that God is going to be pleased with you, then I think you should see a doctor, because those "inner demons" you're struggling with so manfully are really nothing that a twenty dollar whore couldn't put right in a couple of minutes. But of course you couldn't do that, because that would be sinful. Much better to insert your penis into a choirboy, and then carry on lecturing dying Africans on sexual abstinence.

If any cardinals or bishops are watching this video, let me ask you a question. On a theological level, is it more of a sin for a priest to rape a child while wearing a condom, or not wearing one? How much more evil is it to wear the condom? And would it be OK, i.e. would you keep quiet about it, if he went to confession afterwards and truly repented, until the next time?

The Catholic Church has lost so much money on this scandal, they must be down to their last few billion by now. If you were Pope wouldn't it make sense to try and add up all the sex abuse that's been committed so far, and then add up all the money that's been paid out in compensation, and then you might be able to work out exactly how much the Church is paying for, say, one blowjob, and whether it might be more economical to buy the same product from a professional sex worker. That way you'd be helping to employ somebody in a legitimate occupation. Certainly one that's more legitimate than yours is, your holiness, your eminence, your grace.

A little word of advice – clean your own stained glass windows before you start cleaning everybody else's, and then people might take you a little more seriously. Peace.

15

Origin of the Species

June 13, 2007

Where do we come from? This is the ultimate question for us, I suppose, and at the moment we've got two opposing theories. We've got the evolution or the science theory, and the creation or the magic theory. Both equally valid. Both equally plausible. Apparently.

And to emphasise this they've now built a creation museum where all the myths of the Bible can finally come to life a lot more fully than they ever did in the past, for twenty dollars a head.

The creation theory of course comes from the book of Genesis, which tells us God created man from a handful of dust and he created woman from man's rib. And these two together were so stupid that they weren't on the planet five minutes when they'd managed to get a curse put on all future generations. Nice work.

But in a way this is one positive thing about Genesis, that it does give us a kind of status. It confers on us a tragic nobility where we're communing directly with God, wrestling with major themes, and not just grubbing around in the dirt for insects, as we otherwise would have been. So just for our own self-respect, if Genesis didn't exist, we'd have to write it, if somebody hadn't already beaten us to it a few thousand years ago.

Darwin's theory of natural selection, on the other hand, tells us that we have evolved over millions of years from lower life forms such as lizards, apes, and born again Republicans.

And many Christians would like to see both of these theories taught in schools so that kids can get both sides of the argument. But what I don't understand is why there are only two sides to this argument. Why only two theories? Because this is a very important question, so surely we need all the theories we can get, especially as the two we've got are so mutually exclusive. If you embrace one you have to reject the other. What kind of absolutist madness is this? There has to be some middle ground.

(Sound of a police siren in the street)

My cab must be early.

OK, here's a question: If you crossed a pig with a monkey, what would you get? I'll give you a clue. Look in the mirror. Now I'm not trying to be insulting, but it's true, isn't it?

We know that genetically we are very close to monkeys, but we're also very close to pigs, which is great news if you're looking for an organ transplant. In fact, in some cannibal societies human meat is known as long pig.

So maybe here's what happened. A few million years ago a monkey had sex with a pig (I know it's wrong, but they were at a loose end on a Saturday night, these things happen) and they produced the first human, a remarkable creature that could not only peel bananas with its feet but was mustard at sniffing out truffles. And from this we evolved into the articulate dextrous pig-monkeys we are today.

Still not convinced? OK, let's call the monkey Adam, and the pig, oh I dunno, you think of something.

Well, why not? It makes more sense than either of the other theories, as it explains why there's no missing link while eliminating the supernatural, so I'd like to see it taught in schools. Let's give the kids all the available theories, and let them decide.

We are the pig-monkeys of planet earth, this is my theory. And since I don't have a shred of evidence to support it, naturally I believe it all the more passionately. Peace.

16

The Myth of Islamophobia

June 21, 2007

I've had a lot of e-mails from people who seem to think that I hate Muslims, when nothing could be further from the truth, not even the official reason for the war in Iraq, which is about as far from the truth as Pluto is from the sun.

But this illustrates, I think, a quality we have as human beings; we tend to read into a thing what we want to see there, rather than what's actually there, which is of course what makes the so-called holy scriptures so dangerous.

Let me make this crystal clear. I have no problem with Islam, with the Islam where people get on with their lives and pray every day and don't bother anybody else. Nor do I have a problem with any religion that has the common decency to mind its own business.

But that's not the Islam I'm talking about, and I think we all know this. I'm talking about the repressive, violent, intolerant Islam that considers human rights an insult to God, the Islam that wants homosexuals killed along with adulterers and anybody else who thinks they're entitled to a private life.

But I don't hate anyone, because hate is for losers. Hate is just fear with attitude.

If you hate something you're afraid of it, which makes you nothing but a big pussy. And whatever you hate and fear, you know you're going to attract it, because if you invest that much emotion in something, it's coming your way.

The Islamic fundamentalist, he hates America. America is coming his way.

Here in Britain we hate intolerance. Guess what's coming our way.

This week the Queen of England was burned in effigy on the streets of Pakistan. Why? Because she gave a knighthood, a pretty worthless bauble at the best of times, to an author* better known for his nuisance value than for his actual writing. It doesn't mean he has to walk around in a suit of armour, although it might be advisable if he ever goes anywhere near Pakistan, where the government has declared this an insult to Islam. Well, I mean, what isn't these days?

I do find it difficult to take seriously this moral outrage in Pakistan, coming as it does from a country whose attitude to women degrades the entire human race.

The real insult to Islam is the fact in Pakistan a woman can be murdered for the crime of being raped.

The worst thing that can happen to anyone in Pakistan is to

* Salman Rushdie.

be born female. Every year thousands of women in Pakistan are murdered by members of their own family, yet nobody is insulted by that. Nobody is demanding an apology for that.

Instead, what do we get? A deafening silence from Muslims – almost a miracle in itself.

According to the Human Rights Commission of Pakistan, eighty percent of Pakistani women are regularly beaten by their husbands. I mean come on guys, shape up. You can't blame your culture for everything.

And yet these are the people who have accused the British government of Islamophobia. And this must really sting the politically correct religious appeasers who run this country, because they've already done so much to accommodate Islamic sensibilities, even legitimising crackpot pressure groups like the Muslim Council of Britain, who recently issued a list of demands that would impose Islamic values on all children in British schools.

The Muslim Council of Britain sounds like an official body, but in fact it's just another extremist group of fanatics who want to turn Britain into an Islamic republic. They'd never admit this publicly, of course, any more than the British National Party would admit that they want to repatriate the blacks and gas the Jews, but we all know that's where they're really coming from.

And they love accusing people of Islamophobia, a totally made up word, and a blatant lie.

A phobia is defined as an irrational fear or dread of something, and it's true that many people fear and dread the growth of Islam, but there's nothing irrational about that when you look at the evidence. In countries where Islam has control there's repression, there's torture, there's precious few human rights, and there's no free speech. And if the Muslim Council of Britain had its way this would be one of those countries, and I'd be arrested and tortured for making this video. This is not a belief system that I want to see encouraged. But there's nothing phobic about it. It's just common sense.

The real phobia lies with Islam itself, and all religions, with their pathological fear of reason, which they know can evaporate all their delusions in an instant, because reason to religion is like sunlight to a vampire. That's where the real fear is. And that's where the real hate is.

Peace, especially to everyone in the religion of peace.

17

What About the Jews?

June 29, 2007

Hi everybody. I've been asked by a few people why I criticise Muslims and Christians, but not Jews. Well, this is possibly because, of the three dogmas in the children of Abraham – Muslims, Jews and Christians – I like the Jews the best. When I say I like them, I think all three religions are an insult to humanity, but Jews don't do quite as much complaining and privilege-seeking as the other two dogmas. And, more importantly, whereas Muslims and Christians want everybody to believe what they believe, Jews don't give a damn what you believe as long as you leave them alone, and I like that.

On the other hand, I have heard a rumour that Israel is secretly controlled by Jews, and I'm not sure I like the sound of that. I'm talking about proper Jews, obviously, not the ordinary everyday man in the street sort of Jew, but the ultra orthodox hardcore boys who still attack people for whistling or gathering sticks upon the Sabbath. You know, the guys who'd rather they were still living four thousand years ago, apart from a brief excursion into eighteenth-century Russia for some clothes.

And this surprises me. I had always assumed that the Christians were really in charge because they control America, and America controls Israel.

We know, for example, that not all Zionists are Jews. There are a number of influential Christian Zionists who would like nothing better than for the Jews to rebuild their temple in Jerusalem, because they believe that this will herald the second coming of Christ and, as an added bonus, the final destruction of those pesky Christ-killing Jews. That's right, the ones who won't convert, apparently Christ is going to come and show Hitler and the Catholic Church how it should have been done.

Meanwhile the political situation in Israel is like a knotted rope. The harder they try to pull it apart, the tighter it gets. And this is because elements on both sides remain vigilant against any possible outbreak of peace. Islamists on one hand, settlement-building Jews on the other. In other words, the people motivated most strongly by their religious beliefs. What a surprise.

Given the history of the Jews, it's easy to understand why they would want their own autonomous Jewish state, but the problem is it's in the wrong place, because if there was any justice in this world Israel would currently occupy half of Germany. But Israel is not really about justice, is it? It's really about Jerusalem, which is really about scripture and prophecy, which as we know is really about insanity.

Jerusalem, of course, is a sacred city to all three dogmas in the children of Abraham (which frankly is the best argument I've heard for bulldozing the place, pushing all the rubble into the sea, and then sowing salt in the ground so that nothing will grow there for a thousand years) but right now the Jews happen to control it, and the Christians are happy about this because they know how much this pisses off the Muslims.

See, the Christians are taking this opportunity to help rub the Jews in the Muslims' faces, because they haven't forgotten the humiliation they suffered just eight hundred short years ago in the Crusades, and now it's payback time.

And the Jews, they know they're being used like this, of course, but they also know how much the Muslims really hate them being there, and the whole thing presumably appeals to their famous Jewish sense of humour, which it looks like they're going to need, because the president of Iran, Mr Ahmadinejad, appears to have committed himself, not to a mental hospital as you might expect, but to developing nuclear weapons.

He claims his nuclear programme is for peaceful purposes. He doesn't say whether this includes wiping Israel off the map, a desire he has expressed quite forcefully in the past, but I think the Israelis believe it does, and that's really all that matters.

We know Israel has nuclear weapons, and we're pretty sure it would use them if its existence was seriously threatened. So I think we can all safely assume that Israel is not going to disappear any time soon without a nuclear war, which would be a disaster for the Middle East. It would turn the whole region into a desert.

But if Iran is determined to get nuclear weapons, what can we do about it, realistically? I mean what do we do, invade Iran and get bogged down in a long bloody land war with them, when we already know from experience that they've got lots of cannon fodder, I mean people.

And why should we even care, when Israel has ignored so many United Nations resolutions telling them to get out of the occupied territories, which they just can't bring themselves to do because of Jerusalem and the temple and scripture and prophecy, and the fact that they'd have an awful lot of very angry religious Jews on their hands.

Peace in the Middle East, it's a lovely dream in theory, but, as people of the book, we have to live in the real world of miracles and divine revelation, unfortunately. It's just reality, I'm afraid.

I think the Jews would do themselves a huge favour if they came to their senses and let go of Jerusalem. It doesn't belong to them, and they're only holding on to it because of religion, which is the worst possible reason to do anything on this planet.

They say the quickest route between two points is a straight line. Well, it's a straight line between religious politics and bloodshed. Always has been, always will be.

Keep the Jewish state, by all means. I like the Jewish state. I've been there, I like the place, I like the people. But you don't need Jerusalem. You're bigger than that.

The Jewish state has proved itself. It's not to be trifled with. We get that now.

But Jerusalem is not a Jewish town, it's an Arab town. And it's time we all started to acknowledge that and live in reality before reality imposes itself on us in the most unpleasant way imaginable.

So please, Jews, do us all a favour and give it back, and help put a stop to this madness. The whole world will thank you for it. And you know what? You'll probably end up as the most popular people on the planet. And wouldn't that be a turn-up for the books.

Shalom. You know it makes sense.

18

Politics and Religion

July 10, 2007

Somebody asked me this week: "Why do you only talk about religion, and not about other things?"

Well, when you talk about religion you really are talking about other things in the modern world, if you'll pardon that euphemism for what we've actually got.

Indeed, some people even talk about religion now in terms of a clash of cultures, when they say that Islam and democracy don't get along because, like hospitals and health, or like justice and the law, or like Jesus and born again Christians, they've got nothing in common.

I think that politics and religion is an extremely dangerous mixture, because, like sulphur and saltpetre, on their own they're manageable enough, but put them together and you get gunpowder.

And I think this is the reason why, for example, the fanatics who flew into the Twin Towers or the lunatics who blew themselves up in London, although they were politically motivated, they only went through with it because of what they believed about the afterlife, or more exactly, about the unknowable.

And I think this is the danger of religion: it operates in this world of reason, but outside the bounds of reason, which is a polite way of saying outside the bounds of sanity.

Some countries like Iran are governed by religious fundamentalist nutcases. Other countries like Israel and Pakistan owe their very existence to religion.

And of course let's not forget the Vatican, which has a seat at the United Nations because it has somehow managed to persuade people that it's a legitimate country. All the better for stifling any birth control initiatives that may have slipped under the American government's radar.

Without religion, Pakistan and Israel wouldn't exist, and what a sad loss that would be. It would be almost as bad as losing Nigeria, wouldn't it? And there's a country divided by fundamentalist religion. Muslims to the north, Christians to the south – maybe a few Jews in between, but not for long, I'll bet.

As for Pakistan, well that only exists because about sixty years ago in that part of the world Muslims and Hindus just couldn't get along, and they couldn't stop slaughtering each other with machetes for more than five seconds at a time, so the only solution was to start up a whole new country, which is as good as saying: "We can never live together, we'll always be enemies. Let's both build nuclear weapons and see how it goes."

I think it's quite ironic that the first nuclear conflict on this planet could easily erupt between Muslims and Hindus, or between teetotallers and vegetarians.

Clearly red meat and alcohol may be killers, but they're nothing compared with human stupidity. And that's never in short supply, especially where religion is concerned.

For example, how long do we have to wait for a serious American presidential candidate to admit that they don't believe in God. In other words, how long do we have to wait for American politics to grow up? Right now they're all terrified of losing the ignorance vote, because that's the vote that's going to elect the president. And what a wonderful job it did last time.

Of course we can't crow too much in the United Kingdom, because our ex-prime minister, Mr Blair, a man with impeccable Christian credentials, now has a new job as Middle East peace envoy, which is going to mean a few slippery handshakes as he meets people with almost as much blood on their hands as he has.

He's not as popular as he was, Mr Blair, because, having lied as he did in order to invade Iraq with all the gung-ho enthusiasm of somebody who has never seen war and whose own son is not in the firing line, he showed us basically who he is, and now of course he senses our contempt, so it's no wonder he's in denial. You can see it in his eyes. He can't wait to move to America.

Before he resigned, he criticised the British press and compared them to feral beasts. And it's true that the British press can be very irresponsible, but not nearly as irresponsible as the cowardly American press which is so crawlingly supine and unwilling to criticise their stupid and criminal government for fear of appearing unpatriotic that they've literally become a laughing stock all over the world.

I think the British press, though, were actually quite kind to Mr Blair, because any other head of state with his track record they'd be calling to have prosecuted for war crimes.

So I suppose it's grimly appropriate that he's now decided to convert to that traditional friend of the war criminal, the Catholic faith, or the brotherhood of the damned, as I prefer to think it.

No, all in all I think politics and religion are just too closely entwined, and I think we need to prise them apart if civilisation is going to remain on the agenda.

Of course nobody knows what the future holds. You could say it's in God's hands, or Old Butterfingers, as I like to call him.

But the way things are going it might not even get here, because right now we're engaged in a tug of war with the past, and lately it's been digging its heels in. And I think this is one that we really do need to win, because if we lose we're going to find ourselves back in the Dark Ages, where knowledge is a crime and where free speech is blasphemy. And that's really the reason why I talk about religion, and not other things.

Peace and love to one and all, if that's not wishful thinking.

19

Why Does Faith Deserve Respect?

July 19, 2007

Why is faith worthy of so much respect? Would somebody show me the calculations, because I just don't get it.

People keep saying to me: "You should show a bit more respect. You don't have to call people mentally ill just because they disagree with you."

Well, it's not because they disagree with me that I call them mentally ill. It's because of what they believe about reality, and more importantly what they want to do with those beliefs.

If that's all it was, just a belief, then I'd have no problem giving religion all the respect it wants, in the same way that I respect a person's dress sense or the décor in their home. Even if I found it tasteless I would respect them enough not to say so.

But religion is more than just a belief. Religion wants to impose a universal morality, which is why it has always attracted the kind of person who thinks other people's private lives are their business. And giving respect to this mentality is exactly what has got us into the mess that we're in.

We've given religion ideas above its station, and we've persuaded it that it's something it's not, when the truth is that faith is nothing more than the deliberate suspension of disbelief. It's an act of will. It's not a state of grace. It's a state of choice, because without evidence you've got no reason to believe, apart from your willingness to believe. So why is that worthy of respect, any more than your willingness to poke yourself in the eye with a pencil?

And why is faith considered some kind of virtue? Is it because it implies a certain depth of contemplation and insight? I don't think so. Faith, by definition, is unexamined, so in that sense, it has to be among the shallowest of experiences.

And yet, if it could, it would regulate every action, word, and thought of every single person on this planet, because let's not forget, even an impure thought is a sin.

Well, I think that belief in God is an impure thought. It pollutes our understanding of reality. It gets in the way, and it brings out the worst in the best of us, so that we're even prepared to stoop so low as to poison the unformed minds of the people we love the most, our children. By the time they're old enough to think for themselves it's too late. They've been well and truly hypnotised.

I'm sorry, but there's no nice way to say this. If you fill your child's mind with images of Satan and the horrors of hellfire, you're a sick individual, and you are mentally ill.

And the only reason you don't know this is because you've

been indulged for far too long by people and institutions that really ought to know better. The truth is your beliefs are infantile, your scriptures are lies, and your gods are illusions. And I can say that with all due respect, because no respect is actually due.

Besides, anyone who has to demand respect automatically deserves ridicule. If you deserved respect you'd already have it. You'd be rolling around in it like a televangelist in other people's money.

No, what you deserve is mockery. But I'm a reasonable person and I want to make an effort, so I'll tell you what I'll do. I'll respect your beliefs for as long as I can keep a straight face while thinking about them, which should be about half a second, but beyond that I'm afraid I can't promise anything.

In the meantime I don't believe that God exists, but if it turns out that I'm wrong about that, well fair enough. I don't think much of his attitude, to be honest, and if he wants to show himself I'll be happy to tell him that to his face, if he's got one.

But if God exists, I want him to tell me himself. I don't want to hear it from anybody else. And in case you're wondering, that includes you.

So please don't quote any more scripture at me. I'm really up to here with scripture, and frankly I don't give a damn what the Bible or the Koran have to say about anything. You might as well be telling me about your dreams, which is essentially what you are doing.

I can understand why people are drawn to scripture and to religion, because it's so easy and convenient. It's all laid out for you. All the thinking you'll ever need has already been done. You don't have to lift a single braincell. That's so convenient it's almost modern.

But what you've got to realise is believing a thing, no matter how strongly, doesn't necessarily make it real. I mean you can also be hypnotised into believing you're a chicken, but you can't reasonably expect other people to share that belief, at least until they see a few eggs.

And that's the bottom line here – evidence. If you show me a few eggs then I will believe that you are a chicken, or a Christian or a Muslim, or whatever the hell it is you think you are.

But until then, please don't tell me not to mock your beliefs. That's like telling me not to laugh at your toupee. It just makes the damn thing even more ridiculous.

Peace to everyone, and may you get all the respect that you deserve.

20

God Bless Atheism

August 3, 2007

I live in a society where everyone's beliefs are respected, as long as they believe in God.

But, despite that, there are still some good reasons to be an atheist. Personally, I like the hours – twenty-four seven. I find they suit me very well indeed.

People often ask me about being an atheist, and certain questions crop up all the time. For example: "How can you know good from evil without religion to guide you?"

Well, that's just the point, isn't it? Religion does guide me. Most of the things I see religion do I think are evil, and I find that's a pretty useful benchmark. If religion's involved, I know evil won't be too far away.

Another question is: "Isn't atheism itself really just another religion?"

Well, I suppose atheism is a religion in the same way that creationism is a science, or Islam is a religion of peace. In other words, when language no longer really means anything.

How can atheism be a religion? Who do we worship, and who's going to kill us if we don't?

Atheism doesn't demand absolute unquestioning obedience, or make threats about eternal damnation, nor does it take childish offence over trifles.

It doesn't protect sex offenders from justice, nor does it treat women like livestock.

In a way it's a shame it's not a religion, because we might get a few tax breaks out of it. But no, atheism doesn't get any special privileges. There are no schools teaching atheism to children as a belief system, paid for with public money. Nor does atheism require anyone to tithe part of their income to keep a few cynical conmen in luxury.

So you see it doesn't even begin to qualify as a religion worthy of the name.

No, to me atheism is just another word for reality. It simply means not seeing any need to apologise for being human, and to be quite happy to live the life I do have, and not wish it away on some celestial three card trick that tells me: "Heaven is right there waiting for you, and all you've got to do is die."

That's some price to pay for admission to a place which is likely to be full of clergymen and born again Christians, which I reckon makes it literally a fate worse than death.

"But surely people need religion to answer certain questions."

Yes, questions like: How best can we stifle the human spirit? How much can we squeeze from the poor and gullible? And how many palaces can we live in at once without blushing?

These questions religion answers very well indeed.

But unfortunately there are other questions to which it doesn't have answers, so it makes them up. And this is where atheism comes in. Atheism says: "Hey, you just made that up."

And religion says: "No, this is what we call theology."

What's the difference between a doctor of medicine and a doctor of theology? One prescribes drugs, and the other might as well be on drugs.

A theologian is somebody who is an expert in the unknowable, and has all the qualifications to prove it. Yes, a real specialist.

And this is why I think the question we should be asking is not whether atheism is a religion, but why theology is regarded as a branch of philosophy, and not as a creative art? Because it is very creative. You can dress your god up in whatever set of the king's new clothes you like. And that must be great fun for all concerned, but personally I don't see any more reason to teach it in universities than there is to teach astrology.

"OK, we get it, you don't believe in God, but at least religious organisations do a lot of good work, especially in the third world. Surely you can't knock that."

So what are you telling me, if they weren't religious they wouldn't be doing this work? It's not really coming from their hearts? They're just doing it because they're following orders? Is that what you're saying?

I suppose if they were heathen atheists they wouldn't have time to do it, because they'd be too busy debauching and indulging every wicked urge their fevered imaginations could dream up.

Because that's what we atheists do, of course, isn't it? Our souls are corrupted and stained with sin because, well, it's just a great lifestyle, frankly.

In fact, when I finish making this video I intend to spend the rest of the afternoon sinning, because I know I won't be punished for it.

In fact I'm getting so excited about it I think I'll stop right now. So peace to everyone, especially to all heretics, apostates and infidels.

21

Islam in Europe

August 17, 2007

Recent events in Brussels have confirmed for us in Europe what we've long suspected, that we're governed by unprincipled vote-whoring cultural apologists who can't wait to dismantle our heritage in order to show how culturally sensitive they are, and who would be quite happy to see us all living under sharia law as long as it keeps them in office.

As a result, we've got a situation now in Europe – whether it's halal meat for Danish schoolchildren, or German judges quoting sharia law, polygamy legalised in Germany now (for Muslim men only, of course), or an Italian court allowing a Muslim to brutally beat his daughter when anybody else would be imprisoned – Islamic values are now being imported wholesale into Europe and are being imposed on a population to whom they're about as welcome as a melanoma.

No other religion gets these privileges, and some people in Europe are so angry about this creeping Islamisation of their culture that they're starting to protest against it, when they're allowed to. *2007*

Only on September 11th this year in Brussels they won't be allowed to, because a peaceful demonstration intending to mark the anniversary with a minute's silence outside the European parliament has been banned by the mayor of Brussels in case certain members of the religion of peace react violently.

After all, we wouldn't want to offend people who were dancing in the streets on September 11th. That would be disrespectful.

And before somebody decides to call me racist or Islamophobic yet again, you can save your breath. Islamophobia is not the label of shame it might have been, had it been a more honest word. Thanks to radical Islam and its open hatred of everything we stand for, calling somebody in Europe Islamophobic is now more likely to be taken as a compliment than it is as an insult. And our politicians have only got themselves to blame for that, because what they need to realise is that we in Europe reject sharia totally – not because it's different, but because it's barbaric.

We once also employed mutilation and gruesome death in the name of religious justice. We called it the Inquisition. But then we came to our senses. Dare I say it, we became more civilised.

And before somebody reminds me that Islam preserved ancient scientific knowledge when Europe was still going through the Dark Ages, yes, that's very commendable, but you get the impression that Islam wouldn't do that now, because modern Islam, if you'll pardon the expression, seems to be more about bulldozing ancient statues than preserving ancient texts, apart from its own ancient text, of course.

And the results of that are there for all to see in any country where Islam has control; notably in the leading Sunni state, Saudi Arabia, and the leading Shia state, Iran. Both barbaric regimes with brutal Iron Age values. And we don't want that in Europe any more.

I'm sorry to be so racist and Islamophobic and everything, but we've seen how every concession to Islam is the thin end of an even bigger wedge, and we don't want religious police patrolling our streets, not anywhere, for anyone. We don't want legalised rape, amputations, stoning, beheading, or any of the other niceties of Islamic jurisprudence, where a man's word is worth twice that of a woman, as long as he doesn't let on that he's secretly gay, of course. That would be a fly in the ointment. And what a dilemma for the judge. He wouldn't know who to stone to death first.

What I'd like to know from our European politicians if they can spare a couple of seconds to step down off the gravy train, is when will it be time to stop showing respect for Islam? Will it be when they take away your wine and your beer because they disapprove of it, would that do it for you? Or perhaps when your wife is beaten up for showing her face in public? Or maybe you'll wait until your daughter is raped and then punished for it. Would you show less respect then, or would you continue to be culturally sensitive and suck it up like you're sucking it up now?

Because, if that's the case, then my advice to the future people of Europe is: Don't be a woman. And don't even think about being gay.

I wonder how long it will be before the first European is actually stoned to death for adultery. If that catches on there'll be hardly anyone left in France.

Although that's not strictly true, is it, because according to current birthrate projections, France will be a majority Muslim country anyway in about fifty years. But something tells me that nobody will be breaking out any champagne.

Our friends in America have their critics here in Europe, as we know, but I get a lot of e-mails from Americans who think that Europeans are spineless, and I think they're right.

Yes, we confronted Hitler, but only after a lot of hand-wringing. We could see it coming a mile off, but we only acted when we no longer had any choice, and by then it was too late.

To make matters worse, most people living in Europe nowadays have never actually had to fight for the freedom they enjoy, and so I think we've forgotten its true value.

And this is precisely why our politicians feel that they can trade it away so cheaply for the sake of their own miserable careers.

So I say cultural sensitivity be damned. Some things are more important. Peaceful protest and free speech are not negotiable, and anyone who's offended by that can damn well stay offended.

Personal faith should stay personal. It has no place in other people's lives.

Centuries ago religion may have had a role to play in maintaining social order, but now it's a threat to social order. It's a threat to world peace, quite frankly, and I think its role should be seriously reassessed in all civilised countries.

We need to devalue faith as a currency, especially here in Europe, if we're to survive. We need to put a stop to all religious appeasement.

So let's prove the Americans wrong and show them that we do have a spine. We can set them an example of how to get the cancer of religion out of public life for good, because they could certainly use one.

Peace to everyone, especially to the mayor of Brussels and his Muslim constituents who keep him in office, for the time being.

22

Unholy Scripture

August 31, 2007

Hi everyone. I'd like to say a couple of things here. Firstly, about my videos. I post them on various websites, and I appreciate all the comments and messages I get, but I could really do without seeing any more racist comments if you wouldn't mind. I'm speaking here to the white racists, but this applies equally well to the brown ones. I don't share your pathetic obnoxious views in any way imaginable, so if you really have to show the world what an intellectual insect you are please don't do it here, because every time I see one of your comments it's like stepping in dogshit, and I don't want to have to follow you around with a pooper scooper, so if you could help me out and just put them somewhere else, preferably up your own fundament using the business end of a pineapple, I'd be much obliged.

And secondly, I'd like to say a few words about the Bible.

It seems to me that, because faith operates outside the bounds of reason, it feels entitled to claim knowledge from unreasonable sources, such as divine revelation, which is a fancy way of saying voices in the head, or dreams, or even drugs, if you read the Book of Revelation, which is an extraordinary account of a bad trip through the canyons of a frazzled mind.

It's the last book in the Bible, and it was written by John of Patmos. And he was definitely on something, because the island of Patmos is notoriously abundant in psilocybin mushrooms, and you don't need to ingest too many of them to start having rabid visions, maybe even scribble a book of wild ramblings and ravings while you're at it. What could be more natural?

Although, reading Revelation, I don't get the impression of anyone actually having written it so much as shouted it while hanging upside down by his ankle from a bell tower, or scrawling it in his own blood on the city walls.

It's fair to say I'm not entirely convinced that this is the product of a healthy mind.

Of course I have to balance these doubts against the counter argument, which is: "But it's in the Bible, so it must be true, because the Bible is the word of God, because it says it is, so it must be true because the Bible is the word of God..." etcetera, etcetera.

Clearly, for some people, God doesn't move so much in mysterious ways, as in ever decreasing circles.

I wonder if he goes in the opposite direction in the southern hemisphere. Maybe somebody can write and let me know.

I find it quite ironic that some Christians would like to ban the Harry Potter books in case their children turn to witchcraft and away from Jesus, as opposed to turning to Christianity and even further away from Jesus, from what I've seen. Jesus Camp, anyone? I don't know about you, but I smell sulphur.

But you know, I think once you start banning books, you really start banning civilisation. And that's why I would never be in favour of banning the holy scriptures (which is a question I was asked recently) even though I think they do more harm than good.

I think the Bible, and the Koran for that matter, are very ambiguous books to quite a dangerous degree, because they both preach peace, as they often claim to do, yes, but they also preach violence. So really it depends what you're actually looking for when you open the book, because that's pretty much what you're going to find.

And if you choose to read it literally, well then yes, you've got yourself a charter for barbarism. But if you approach it as the inspirational text it was doubtless meant to be, you can access a world of subtlety and wisdom.

But you have to actually want to do it, and unfortunately too many people prefer dogma to enlightenment. They'd rather use their holy books to reinforce their own narrow prejudices and then try to impose them on everybody else. Like cavemen using a flashlight as a hammer, they've missed the point completely. And for me this is the most depressing thing about the holy scriptures.

But, since we are using them to lay down rules of behaviour for other people, it's clear to me from the New Testament that anyone who goes to church on Sunday is a blasphemer, because Jesus specifically said don't pray in public, keep your religion to yourself, didn't he? In the Sermon on the Mount, I think it was, Matthew 6, verses 5 and 6.

Don't be like the hypocrites, he said, who pray in the synagogues and on street corners where they can be seen. No no, not you. You go into your closet and shut the door, and pray to God in secret, and God will hear you in secret and reward you openly.

That's what he said. Keep your religion to yourself. It's right there in black and white in the Queen's English in the Holy Gospel. How much more true could it possibly be?

Clearly, therefore, every Christian church is nothing but a halfway house on the road to hell.

And don't blame me. I didn't say it. The Bible did.

Peace, and all that jazz.

23

Video Response to Osama

September 11, 2007

Well, this week we've heard from the Antichrist in waiting, Osama bin Laden, who wants everyone in the West to convert to Islam to stop the war in Iraq. Well, that sounds very realistic, doesn't it? I'm glad to see he hasn't lost his mind sitting up there in his little cave.

Osama, if you're watching, thanks for the offer, but no thanks. There's no way that I could ever convert to Islam, for a number of reasons. Firstly, I like beer. Now I know that sounds very hedonistic and shallow, but, as you know, it's part of my culture to be hedonistic and shallow. Also, in my culture right now it's become very fashionable to respect everyone's cultural values, no matter how crude or barbaric or downright ridiculous they might be, and this is something which you and your Islamist friends have capitalised on with great success in recent years.

And yet you still don't seem to approve, and I find that

disappointing. To you, western society, or the Zionist Crusader Alliance (let's give it its official title) is still an abomination which must be destroyed. It's decadent and immoral; there's too much sex, too much music, too much laughter, there's just too much fun, isn't there, Osama? And you want to put a stop to it before you have a brain haemorrhage.

To you, western women are whores, because they show far too much flesh for your liking, and I bet that brings you out in a hot flush just thinking about it all the time.

In fact, that's another reason that I couldn't possibly convert to Islam. Anyone who seriously expects me to stand by while the women in my life are compelled to dress or behave in a way they consider inappropriate is, frankly, living in a fantasy world. But then we already knew that, didn't we?

As for Iraq, you know as well as I do that virtually everybody on the planet wants the troops out of Iraq now, except for the idiot in the White House, the same one that you helped get re-elected, by the way, the last time you popped up on our screens, remember, you interfering son of a bitch?

Because the truth is you wanted the war to continue every bit as much as he did. You wanted Muslims slaughtered and at each others' throats, purely to embarrass the Americans, which is all you really care about, isn't it, you hypocrite?

You know, Osama, there are over a billion Muslims living on this planet, and I think every single one of them should be cursing you for what you've done to their religion, because you've actually achieved the impossible – you've set Islam back several hundred years, so that even for someone like me making this video it's very difficult not to resort to obscenities, especially when there's more obscenity in what you stand for than I could possibly generate in cursing you and all your worthless ancestors back to the year dot, you cowardly violent scumbag, you self-righteous piece of shit.

But hey, I don't want to get abusive here, because that creates enemies. On the other hand, you're already my enemy, so what the hell, you murdering lump of slime.

However, I want to make it very clear that the idiot in the White House is also my enemy, just in case you thought I was taking sides. Of course he's a much bigger enemy to the troops he actually sent to Iraq. In fact he's probably the greatest enemy they've got. He's also now an enemy to his own people, thanks to you and your activities, Osama, on this very day six years ago when you deliberately attacked civilians like the unprincipled oil slick you are.

Now, thanks to the sacred war on freedom, I mean terror, America has something called the Patriot Act, which is essentially a charter for fascism in the land of the free.

It could have been written by Hitler, somebody with whom I think you would have a lot in common. After all, a bunker or a cave. Ultimately there's only one way out, isn't there?

Anyway, Osama, I can't stay around chatting all day. I just wanted to say thanks for the offer, but, as you can see, it would be impossible for me to become a Muslim, even if I wanted to. How fortunate for me that I don't want to.

Besides, you know what? I think I'd probably be a bit of a Catholic Muslim, if you know what I mean, and what a combination that would be, eh? Look out Jews. Only kidding, Jews. It was a joke.

Peace everyone, that's all we really want, isn't it? Well, most of us.

24

Hello Angry Christians

September 25, 2007

Hi everyone. I'd like to thank all the angry born again Christians who have been writing to tell me how much they're looking forward to my eternal torment in the flames of hell. It's nice to know that I'm in your prayers.

And you are rubbing your hands with gleeful anticipation, too, some of you, by the sounds of it, when you're not furiously typing pages and pages of scripture. And yet if I call you crazy, apparently I'm the one who's being offensive. It's a funny old world, isn't it?

To be fair, I do actually sympathise to some extent. It must be quite galling for religious people to see atheists like me going about their business without a shred of guilt or self-loathing, and not in the least inclined to pray or do penance of any kind, and not in the slightest bit worried about any form of eternal punishment. I have to admit if I was religious I'd probably think to myself: "How come I've got all this weight on my shoulders while these bums are getting a free ride?"

And I don't even think that I'd be comforted either, as some of you clearly are, by the prospect of their eternal torture in the flames of hell, roasting in agony and tormented by demons, because I don't really buy that scenario. I think if hell does exist it's probably not a place where you physically burn forever, but perhaps a metaphor for something more subtle that consumes from within. Something like eternal regret, perhaps. Something not done, not challenged, not risked, not loved enough. Or maybe it's just burning in fire. I don't want to get heavy about it.

I mean it's bad enough that Jesus died for my sins – I still haven't really gotten over that. (And thanks for reminding me about that yet again, by the way.) I do feel somewhat guilty that I'm not more grateful to Jesus, but I just wish he had taken the trouble to ask me before he went ahead with it, because now I feel I'm being billed for something I didn't order.

And that really is the deal, isn't it, if you're a Christian. You're born already in debt to Jesus, and it's a debt you can only repay in full by dying.

That's some deal you've got yourself into there. That's like being asked to pay off the mortgage on a house that you already own.

Especially as there's no hard historical evidence that the Jesus of the Gospels even existed. What records we do have were written by people who were born long after he died, so they were just passing on what they had heard.

And of course the same is true of the Gospels themselves.

Curious, isn't it, that nobody who was actually writing anything down at the time appears to have known anything about Jesus, despite the fantastic miracles he was performing, the multitudes he was preaching to, and of course his momentous and spectacular public demise.

And don't forget this is a guy whose birth was marked by a celestial event, who was born by a miracle to a virgin in the year 6 BC – two miracles for the price of one, talk about hit the ground running! And then it was one miracle after another; fed the multitude, healed the sick, walked on water, raised the dead, was nailed to a plank and came back to life again. How can nobody have heard of him? He should have been the talk of the desert. He should have been as famous as Elvis.

And yet all we've got is hearsay; second and third hand accounts which have been doctored and edited and translated through a hedge backwards so many times that the truth no longer even bears any resemblance to itself, if it ever did.

So I don't know who you think you're praying to, but it doesn't seem to have done you much good, does it? Maybe you should try praying to Elvis for a while, see how that works out. I mean at least we know that Elvis actually existed.

But just because Jesus is a storybook character that doesn't mean he's not a good character. It doesn't mean he hasn't got wisdom to impart.

Didn't he say the kingdom of heaven is within? Luke 17, verse 21, I think it was. And what a useful piece of information that is when you think about it. Now I realise that, as an angry Christian, you probably pay lip service to those words, but you don't really believe them, and so, for you, it doesn't happen. And clearly it hasn't happened, otherwise you wouldn't be so angry, would you?

Turn the other cheek, forgive trespasses, love your enemy? That's a foreign language to you. No, you want punishment, don't you? You want eternal torture. You want unimaginable suffering, for your own satisfaction.

So I think it's probably just as well that Jesus didn't exist, because if he came back and he saw what people like you have made of his teachings, he'd quickly realise that nobody has listened to a word he said, that he was wasting his breath, and that he'd wasted his life.

Oh well, we've all got our cross to bear.

Peace to everyone, especially Christians, both inside and outside the kingdom of heaven.

25

More Demands from Islam

October 9, 2007

Well, it's a gloomy rainy old day to be here in London, but it could be worse – I could be in Saudi Arabia, where men are men and women are cattle. Can I say that?

The Saudi Arabian Human Rights Commission, now there's a collection of words to boggle the mind, but apparently this organisation does actually exist, and they intend to complain later this month at an event in Copenhagen that Muslims living in Europe are denied human rights and are not allowed to freely practise their faith.

How about that? Being lectured in human rights by Saudi Arabia. What's next, animal welfare from the Koreans? Does it get much more surreal? you ask. Well, yes, apparently it does. Because they also want us to stop linking Islam with terrorism, which is pretty rich coming from the guardians of Islam and the guardians of terrorism.

In a sane society, the guy who actually stands up to make this speech would be bum-rushed out the door the moment he opened his mouth. Or even better, run out of town on a rail and dumped in the river.

But this is Europe, so instead we'll probably listen to what he's got to say and take it all on board, and then change our way of doing things, as usual.

Just this week in the UK we've been told that a leading supermarket chain is now allowing Muslim checkout staff not to handle alcohol if they don't want to. So you can bet your life they'll now be lining up around the block to not want to. We've had a pharmacist refusing to sell birth control because of religion; we've had a Muslim dentist who refused to treat a woman because she wasn't wearing a headscarf, and now we've been told that some Muslim doctors are refusing to treat certain people because of their precious faith.

Well, here in the UK we have a technical term for this kind of behaviour. We call it taking the piss. And we don't like people taking the piss. It gets up our nose, and it gives us the right hump. (It's a cultural thing.)

If Muslims are really as downtrodden as the Saudis would like us to believe, why are there currently plans for a Saudi funded gigantic mosque to be built right here in London? The largest mosque in Europe, no less. (Eat your heart out, Denmark; we know you'd love to have it, but we're getting it instead.) And it's going to be built right next to the site for the 2012 Olympic Games, if they can get planning permission.

Even some local Muslims have been protesting about this plan. They say they'll be marginalised because this mosque will be run by extremists for extremists, which means it's pretty much guaranteed to get the go ahead, and the London Olympics will doubtless be dominated by a mosque the size of a football stadium.

I don't know if the marathon will be interrupted for prayers, or if female athletes will be required to compete wearing a tent, though I'm sure if the mad mullah of multiculturalism, Ken Livingstone,* the mayor of London, has anything to do with it, that won't be too far off the agenda.

The fact that the Saudis feel they can get away with this cynical bullshit just shows how far we've already allowed ourselves to be pushed here in Europe.

Radical Islam has seen us for what we are, a soft touch. It sees that political correctness is like a drug that we just can't stop injecting, even though we know it's going to kill us. And they're taking full advantage of that, turning our sense of fairness against us, and making us despise ourselves for one of our best qualities.

And any concession made will be seen as a sign of weakness to be exploited further, because there is no dialogue with radical Islam. It doesn't want to be agreed with. It wants to be obeyed. It thinks it has the God-given right, aptly enough, to make the rules, not just for Muslims, but for everyone. And some of us, frankly, think that's a little bit too much to ask. And if you think that's unreasonable, all I can say is my freedom is more important than your faith. Much, much more important.

* Thankfully, he was voted out in 2008.

And besides, I just have this natural aversion to being bullied and pushed around by bigoted misogynistic ignoramuses, and I say that with all due respect.

And before somebody accuses me again of insulting Islam, please grow up. I don't need to insult Islam when there are already so many Muslims willing to do it for me every time they strap on a suicide belt or stone somebody to death for the crime of having a private life. These are the people who insult Islam, not people like me.

Of course I realise Islamofascists take pretty much every criticism as an insult by default. But to be fair to them, it would be difficult to think of a compliment, wouldn't it? What do you say? "Nice jihad. Like the dogma. Way to go with the bigotry and hate." There's not much scope really, is there?

But these are the people who are actually insulting Islam. And these are the true enemies of Muslims.

And the biggest enemy of all is the royal family of Saudi Arabia, because it's thanks to their activities, funding and encouraging cold blooded murder in the name of religious dogma, that Islam is feared and resented all over the civilised world, not because of people like me. And the Muslim population needs to take that fact on board and recognise it.

As for us in the West, well, our good friends the Saudis are waging war against us, and we're so fat and complacent we don't even know it. So maybe we deserve everything we get.

People have said to me: "You know, you're pronouncing that wrong. It's not Sordi, it's Sowdi."

Well, OK, fair enough, I'm happy to pronounce it Sowdi. I'd

be even happier if the country was just called Arabia, and the medieval wackos who currently run it were back in the desert living in their tents with their livestock where they belong.

In fact, I'm looking forward to the day when we finally wean ourselves off oil altogether and pull out of the Middle East, and then Sordi and Sowdi Arabia can quietly revert back into the Stone Age, unless they manage to exploit their other great natural resource and start exporting egg timers.

Now that might even be something worth praying for. Peace.

26

What's Good About Religion?

October 23, 2007

If you believe, as I do, that the purpose of religion is to suck all the pleasure out of life and spit it in your eye, then you might have trouble thinking of anything positive to say about it. But I think it's important to try, if just for a sense of balance, so that's why I've decided to think of one or two nice things that I can say about each of the main religions, in particular the three monotheistic dogmas which have plagued... I mean enriched, our civilisation for so many centuries. The three desert dogmas, as I like to think of them, because between them they've done so much to make a desert of the human soul.

Let's begin with Islam. Now in the current climate of intimidation and special pleading you might think it would be hard to say anything nice about Islam, but I can think of a couple of things. Firstly, I like their symbol, the crescent moon. I find it much more attractive than the cross, possibly because it doesn't have anybody nailed to it.

Also, whenever you see film of a large mosque full of worshippers praying together, I like the synchronised bowing. I think that's always very well done.

Also, of course, we have radical Islam to thank for showing us so graphically what a huge problem religion can become. If not for all the hysterical self-righteous bullying that we've been subjected to in recent years, many of us might still be labouring under the illusion that religion is relatively harmless. So thanks to radical Islam for the heads up on that one.

What I like most about Christianity is that it's not Islam, which is a major bonus in my opinion. Unfortunately it is Christianity, which kind of takes most of the shine off it for me.

I like the fact that the Inquisition is over, and that Christian history is no longer being written in blood. I think that's quite a positive development

And recently the Vatican hosted a conference on astronomy, which is quite remarkable, given their track record in that area. I mean it was only a few years ago that the Catholic Church finally got around to admitting that Galileo may be right after all about the earth travelling around the sun.

And that, too, was a very positive thing, because they didn't have to say anything. They could have just kept it quiet, and then millions of Catholics would have been none the wiser.

And of course you can understand why it took them five hundred years to get around to it. With a question of that importance they wouldn't want to rush into any hasty judgments and risk making fools of themselves.

What do I like about Judaism? Well, not a great deal, to be

perfectly honest, except for the fact that it doesn't preach itself into your face every chance it gets, which I think is a very underrated quality, and one which should be widely imitated.

Also of course the Jews have got the oldest of the three dogmas, yet they're the ones who are still waiting for their messiah. And you just know damn well that if he did turn up they'd nail him up for blasphemy again, which is an idea that has always quite amused me, because one thing we should remember is that religion can be a source of great humour, as well as great tragedy, guilt, self-loathing, fear, misery, cruelty, and pain.

Outside of the Abrahamic triangle of insanity, what I like about Hinduism is that they're vegetarians, which I think is a very civilised way to be. (I think they go a little overboard with the cows, but that's their business.) But mainly because Hinduism is not actively trying to take over the world in the way Islam is, and I think that's a very attractive quality in any religion that's nine hundred million strong.

As for Buddhism, well what can I say? A religion with no god. Magnificent. Like a prison with no walls.

So you see, there are plenty of positive things that you can find to say about religion if you look for them.

Now you can say to me: "Well, OK, this is all well and good; you're clearly making an effort to be positive here, but the fact remains that religion is really just a hedge against death. It's an expensive insurance policy which will disappear in a puff of smoke the moment you try to claim on it." And yes, you may well be right about that.

In fact, you might even further argue that anyone who gets their morals unquestioningly from some ancient text might as well get their personality from a microchip. And again I'd find it hard to argue with that point of view.

Religion, you tell me, doesn't have any answers because it doesn't ask any questions; you've rejected it time and time again but it won't take no for an answer, and you don't want to be nice about it any more. You're sick to your back teeth of hearing about people's beliefs and their gods and their scriptures and their precious goddam faith, and you wish that they would take their ridiculous superstitions, and all their cruel and petty stupid little rules and regulations and shove them where the sun doesn't shine. Some kind of black hole, perhaps, is what you've got in mind. And I can certainly relate to that.

I don't like the arrogant way they try to force their narrow prejudices into other people's lives any more than you do, but come on, this is supposed to be a positive video, and I don't want to ruin it by dwelling on the negative things – the selective reasoning, the wishful thinking, and the shameless abandonment of personal responsibility that religious belief embraces in such a self-deceptive and cowardly way. I'd rather focus on the positive.

And the most positive thing I can think of to say, and this is something many believers have said to me as well, is that religion gives people hope; it gives them optimism for the future.

And that is definitely a very good thing. In fact it's something I can certainly relate to, because even after centuries of repression and bigotry and downright bloody minded stupidity,

I'm still optimistic enough to believe that religion is just too absurd to last forever, and that sooner or later humanity's collective intelligence will rise just enough for us to see it for what it actually is, a cruel and manipulative hoax which sustains itself, not by exalting the human spirit, but by breaking it.

And I just hope that when that day arrives we're big enough to laugh at ourselves, because laughter is the best medicine, as we know, even according to the Bible:

"A merry heart doeth good like a medicine, but a broken spirit drieth the bones." Proverbs 17 verse 22.

Peace, especially to everybody with dry bones.

27

Was Jesus Gay?

November 2, 2007

I've had a couple of e-mails from people who want my opinion as to how they should break the news to their fundamentalist Christian parents that they don't believe in God.

Well, the obvious answer is tell them you're gay, and then when they've recovered from the fainting fit and you've administered the smelling salts you can tell them you were only joking, you're not gay, you're just an atheist. And they'll be so relieved they'll sing hallelujah.

Religion doesn't much like gay people, does it? But then of course religion doesn't much like anything. And if we listed all the things religion disapproves of we'd probably still be here next Tuesday. However, it does seem to hold a special place of condemnation in its hard little heart for homosexuals.

To the religious mind, if you're gay, then you've got something wrong with you. Whereas to my mind, if you think it's some kind of insult to call somebody gay, well that's when you've actually got something wrong with you.

It is one of the most common insults I get, and it's also one of the most puzzling, because if I was gay I wouldn't think it was anything to be ashamed of, and even though I'm not, I don't feel in the least bit insulted at being called gay, so what the hell, go ahead and knock yourselves out.

I realise that this is a sensitive subject to some people. Here in the UK we recently had Catholic adoption agencies actually threatening to close themselves down rather than place children with gay parents. Although, given the Catholic Church's record with children, I'd have thought gay parents would be the least of the kids' worries.

The Anglican Church is on the verge of splitting over this issue, because some people don't want gay clergy. And I can understand that. I don't want them either, but then I don't want any kind of clergy.

In America there's a well known televangelist who apparently hates gay people so much he couldn't wait to get his hands on one of them, even paying money for the privilege. Of course he kept it quiet for as long as he could because Christianity and homosexuality make uneasy bedfellows, if you'll pardon the expression, because of course it is an abomination unto the Lord, isn't it? Homosexuality, I mean, not Christianity, obviously. You wouldn't call that an abomination, would you? A laughable parody of Christ's message, perhaps, and a tasteless burlesque of everything he ever stood for, certainly, but an abomination? Oh all right, you've talked me into it. It's an abomination. I was just trying to be nice.

I've heard it suggested from some people that Christians are so irrationally obsessed with this subject because deep down they're terrified that Jesus himself might have been gay.

There's no real evidence for it, but then there's no real evidence for anything to do with religion, so yeah, I'll buy it. Well, keep an open mind, that's what I always say. What do you always say?

To be fair, according to some accounts like the Gospels of Philip or Thomas, it's probable that Jesus wasn't gay, because he got married and had a child. But unfortunately those Gospels never actually made it into the New Testament, so they can't possibly be true.

If we take the actual Gospels as gospel, then what we've got is a man in his thirties, unmarried in a culture where it's almost unheard of for a man of thirty to be unmarried. Plus, come on, you can't ignore the twelve boyfriends, especially when there's a missing passage from the Gospel of Mark that actually describes Jesus spending a night with a naked youth. We're told that the youth came to Jesus wearing a linen cloth over his naked body, and he stayed with him that night, for Jesus taught him the mystery of the kingdom of God. I bet he did, along with one or two other little mysteries while he was at it. Well, why not? He was only human.

The apostle John repeatedly refers to himself as the one who Jesus specially loved. I don't know whether he meant it in the Greek manner, so to speak, but what would it matter if he did? This is the point. If Jesus was gay, would it negate the teachings and the parables? Would the Sermon on the Mount lose its authority if preached by the queen of queens rather than the king of kings?

And if somebody could prove historically beyond all doubt that Jesus was in fact homosexual, would Christians then reject Jesus, or would they reject the evidence as usual? Your guess is as good as mine.

From what I've read in the Gospels I think Jesus was a pretty common sense sort of person, and I don't think he would have had a problem with anybody being who they are. I do think, though, that he had a problem with people who pretend to be one thing, while being another.

So if you are a closet homosexual family man with your own ministry, as I know some of you are, don't be ashamed. God knows you've got enough to be ashamed of without adding imaginary crimes to the list.

It's not a sin to be gay. It's a sin, if anything, to be a liar and a hypocrite about it. So why not do yourself and everyone around you a favour, step out of that closet and show a little pride in who you really are.

Some people won't like it, of course they won't, but you know how bigoted they are. You know that better than anybody.

And anyway you can ignore their opinion because now you'll have the kind of strength that only comes from being true to yourself, and who knows, it might even help to enhance your faith if you take comfort from the real possibility that your messiah, Mr Jesus Christ, was a normal healthy homosexual just like you. Everyone's a winner.

Peace to all Christians, especially the secretly queer ones.

28

A Word to Islamofascists

November 14, 2007

OK, I'd like to say something about the Muslim Council of Britain, whose leader recently accused the security services here of increasing tensions in society by fostering a negative image of Muslims, which is pretty ironic given that the Muslim Council of Britain itself is probably the most high profile negative image there is of Muslims in this country, apart from the actual suicide bombers.

Of course there are various ways that you can increase tensions in society; not least people who constantly push for unwarranted religious privilege, and who issue lists of demands that would impose Islamic values on every school in Britain.

People who refer to themselves as community spokesmen when they actually speak for nobody but themselves and their Wahhabi fundamentalist paymasters in Saudi Arabia, where just last week somebody was actually executed on suspicion of practising witchcraft.

Intolerant misogynists who are given a free platform to insult this country during Remembrance Week by comparing Britain with Nazi Germany, in a tasteless and calculated slur guaranteed, and doubtless intended, to insult and offend every grieving war widow in the land.

They also want a ban on alcohol in public and a more modest dress code for everybody, whether they're Muslims or not, and whether they like it or not. How inclusive. How thoughtful.

This organisation, like its American equivalent CAIR, or the Council on American-Islamic Relations, is the "respectable" face of terrorism in the West. The sort of society they'd like to create already exists in Saudi Arabia, where children are raised to hate Jews and to refer to them as vermin and pigs and apes; where young men are so sexually repressed by their religion they spend all their time furiously masturbating over violent internet pornography like a bunch of Catholic priests, and where women have to be invisible in public to avoid being raped.

So you can see why we in Britain might be a little hesitant about welcoming these kinds of values into our society.

But of course this hasn't prevented our spineless government from pandering to these fanatics at every opportunity, most recently promising state-funding for hundreds more Islamic schools, thus encouraging segregation and separation in society, and sowing the seeds of conflict for future generations to have to deal with. They might as well be putting lead in the water supply, and they know it.

It would be easy to blame this on misguided political correctness, but this is actually cynical political opportunism. The truth is the Muslim vote is just too important to lose in places where the Labour Party needs to win. So as usual they're happy to inflict long term damage to achieve short term ends.

They even gave a knighthood to the previous head of the Muslim Council of Britain, despite his public pronouncement that death was too good for Salman Rushdie. They gave him a knighthood anyway for the sake of community relations.

You know what's good for community relations? People who come to this country and who adapt happily to our way of life, or, if they find that it's not quite to their taste, they piss off and live somewhere else. That's really good for community relations.

If you don't like how we do things in Britain, get out. You weren't invited here, and you're not wanted here.

And please don't lecture us on moral values. When you can't even bring yourselves to condemn stoning as a punishment, it's clear that yours is the morality of the cave man.

And for your information, we do have strong moral values in Britain; we just don't feel the need to enforce them with an iron rod because we're not as insecure as you are, and because we believe people should be free to make their own choices in life and not be dictated to by small-minded medievalists who despise everything this country stands for.

And by the way, this has got nothing to do with immigration. Let me make this very clear. I welcome immigration to Britain. I think that within reason it's a healthy thing for the economy, I think it's a good thing for the country. This is about religion, and only about religion.

So to any white supremacist morons out there who think they

can latch on to this video in the way they've attempted to with some of my previous videos, go and take a piss on a live electric rail, because I'm not your friend. I'm your enemy. And I'm proud to be your enemy, just as I'm proud to be the enemy of every creepy Islamofascist on this planet, because you people are two sides of the same coin, and it's an evil worthless poisonous currency that I want nothing to do with.

As for the Muslim Council of Britain, if you insist on shoving your religion into people's faces all the time you shouldn't be surprised to get it shoved right back at you, because that's how we do things in a free society, and if you don't like that you know what you can do.

The people of Britain know damn well that the reason for tensions in our society is nothing to do with the security services or the police, and everything to do with the activities of people like you, the true enemies of Muslims in this country, because every time you open your mouths you make things worse for Muslims. You increase the tension, you increase the resentment. And this is deliberate on your part, because you want Muslims to be in conflict with people all the time in an attempt to intimidate us into allowing you to impose your narrow beliefs and your barbaric values on our society. Well you can whistle up your sawn-off trouser leg for that one my friend, because it's not going to happen. Not now, not ever.

And as for accusing us of being like the Nazis, that really is pretty rich when it's clear that if people like you ever did achieve the kind of universal power you crave, there would be another Holocaust, and everybody knows it.

So we in Britain are going to carry on living the way we like, regardless of what you think about it. We're going to carry on treating women as human beings, and not as possessions. We'll drink alcohol in public if we damn well feel like it, regardless of your sensibilities, and we'll walk around dressed any way we choose. And you might as well get used to it, because if you don't you're going to have a miserable time here, because you're always going to be in conflict. And maybe that is what you want, but I don't think it's what most Muslims want.

To my mind, if religion has a legitimate purpose, it's not as a vehicle for conquering and subduing people as you seem to believe, but as a personal means – and I do mean personal – as a personal means to achieving a peaceful heart, which is, I think, its only legitimate purpose.

And a religious person who is in constant conflict is clearly not even looking for a peaceful heart, and is therefore abusing their religion, and by extension abusing the people who follow that religion, the very people you claim to speak for, you liars, you hypocrites, you duplicitous, mealy-mouthed, unprincipled terrorist-sympathising scum.

Thank you for your time. I'd wish you peace but you wouldn't know what to do with it.

29

Why Debate Dogma?

November 27, 2007

I've had quite a large response to my video about the IslamoNazis who are attempting to drive a fundamentalist wedge into British society with the connivance of our corrupt dhimmi politicians, and some of the most positive messages I got were actually from Muslims who are themselves embarrassed by the activities of these people, so that was very gratifying, and thank you very much indeed for all those.

Inevitably there was plenty of negative feedback as well, from the usual religious nutjobs, but also from some atheists who have told me that they think I'm giving atheism a bad name. Yeah, right. Like it ever had a good name.

I've been told things like my arguments are too crude, I'm damaging the atheist cause, I'm not contributing to the debate, and my personal favourite: "You won't convert anyone to atheism by insulting people."

Well, OK. First of all, as regards being crude. We are talking here about religion, in case you hadn't noticed, and it doesn't come any cruder than monotheistic dogma. I can only aspire to that level of crudity. But just for your sake I promise to do my very best.

Obviously I'd like to show more respect for people's sincerely held beliefs, of course I would, but unfortunately that would violate my own sincerely held belief that religion is a filthy lie and a threat to civilisation. So you can see the problem I've got with that.

Besides, I don't think I'm insulting anyone who doesn't deserve it a thousand times over. I also think if we did a bit more insulting and a bit less pointless debating, then religion might not have such a falsely inflated idea of its own importance, and there might not be so many people on this planet who want us all to live our lives according to ideas and stories that would embarrass a second rate fantasy novelist.

I think to engage dogma in debate is to legitimise it and to confer on it a status that it simply doesn't deserve.

With its arrogant intrusiveness I think it long ago forfeited any claim it may have had to be treated with respect. Too many liberties have already been taken.

Religious dogma has been allowed to encroach on ground it has no right to occupy, and to claim authority where it has no authority to claim anything. And I don't think this is a matter for polite debate, especially when all you're going to get is the usual raft of glibly held but unexamined certainties hammered home like coffin nails at every opportunity, because dogma is blind and deaf to anything reason has to offer. Faith is non-negotiable. So where exactly is the debate?

You obey the rules of reason. Religion ignores them, and neutralises your argument before you've even opened your mouth. It's not interested in anything you've got to say. It's just waiting for you to draw breath so it can say: "Yes, that's all very well, but you've still got to submit, because it's written in this book."

Right now in the UK some Christian fanatics are attempting to take out a prosecution for blasphemy against the producers of a popular comic opera.

Now the very idea of blasphemy, the idea that blasphemy even exists as a concept says it all for me about religion, because what this really means is that some human beings have taken it upon themselves to feel insulted on God's behalf. They don't trust God to decide for himself whether to be insulted and to deal with the matter in the appropriate way on Judgment Day. No, they want to see punishment dished out right here on earth for their own satisfaction. Because it's not really about God, is it? It's really about them and their personal mental illness, as it so often is when religion is exploited and misused by pig-ignorant narrow-minded zealots.

This is the same mentality that wants to compel us all to live in the past. And the past has plenty to teach us, but I don't think it should be allowed to detain us against our will.

Freedom from religion, from other people's unprovable beliefs, is our basic human right. At least I think it is. And some very determined people would like to take that right away from us. And if we don't do anything about that they're going to be allowed to succeed.

Maybe you think the way to deal with this is to engage it in polite debate, and to make all your little points and counterpoints and show us all what a clever dick you are, and that'll be great fun for you. And the good news is you don't even have to worry about somebody like me coming along and damaging your cause, because you haven't got a cause – what you've got is a hobby.

If God existed, and if I had any reason to ask him for anything, I think I'd probably ask him to save me from the curse of polite and deferential atheists.

Religion is out of control right now precisely because too many people have been too diplomatic for too long. If we'd had the balls to do some straight talking years ago when we should have, and put this insulting nonsense in its rightful place with astrology and palmistry, we wouldn't even be talking about this now. We'd be doing something more useful with our time. What a waste of an Enlightenment.

So my position is pretty clear. Believe whatever you want, but if you want me to believe it, then provide evidence or expect mockery and ridicule. Do not expect polite debate.

I'm not trying to convert anyone to anything. I don't give a damn what anyone believes as long as I don't have to keep hearing about it. And by the way, that would include condescending atheists, just for future reference.

I'm not interested in arguing about whether God exists or not. I couldn't give a shit. If he does, he can go and suck eggs for all I care. In fact, he can know himself in the biblical sense, because I want nothing to do with any god who would encourage murder on his behalf, which the god of the desert repeatedly does. In fact, I'm ashamed and embarrassed to have been created by somebody with such moronic values, which is why you'll never hear me bragging about it.

So I'll carry on giving his so-called religion the verbal finger, and you can carry on with your polite discourse, and who knows, maybe you'll come to some kind of amicable compromise where you only have to spend half your life on your knees – that might work for you. And if not, well, at least you'll have something to keep you occupied, which is the main thing really, isn't it?

OK, that's enough. I'm out of here. Peace and love to one and all.

30

Laugh at Sudan

December 3, 2007

Well, it's another public relations triumph for Islam. I was wondering when the angry street mob would appear, I must admit. Who'd have thought it would happen right after prayers? What could they have been listening to?

The government of Sudan has come in for quite a lot of criticism over this,* but apart from shaming their country, debasing their religion, and insulting their Prophet, I think they've handled it rather well, certainly by their usual standards. At least nobody has been massacred yet, which is a step in the right direction.

Of course we were all hoping they would come to what's left of their senses and admit that this was just an innocent misunderstanding, but, as we know, they chose to misunderstand the misunderstanding and make fools of

---

* The Sudanese authorities arrested teacher Gillian Gibbons for allowing children to name a teddy bear "Mohammed".

themselves, embarrassing their own people, and turning their country into a laughing stock. I bet they're even laughing at them in Pakistan over this one. Maybe even in Saudi Arabia. Actually, no. In Saudi Arabia they'd probably execute the teddy bear.

Why they let this happen I really don't know. Maybe they felt they weren't getting quite enough contempt for their unparallelled record of murdering their own people in Sudan.

Maybe they weren't happy with just being known as the genocide capital of the world, and they wanted to get a little bit more attention, just to show themselves off properly in all their full three-dimensional bollock-brained stupidity.

To be fair, the government probably would have let this slide, but for the influence of some hardline clerics who insisted on dragging their religion into the dirt and insulting their own Prophet by using his name to score what everyone can see is nothing but a cheap and grubby political point.

And they've got the nerve to talk about inciting religious hatred, these spiritual vampires, when they're the ones who have been preaching up this storm of hate, demanding that she be publicly executed to make an example of her, when all they've really done is to make an example of themselves, and it's the usual example, the classic combination of cowardice and cruelty we've seen time and again embarrass and disgrace the Islamic religion.

This has done their faith more damage than a thousand blasphemies a million times over, but they're too thick to realise it.

Human nature being what it is, you just can't help wondering now how many pet dogs in the West, or even pot-bellied pigs, have found themselves renamed overnight from Patches or Trixie or Gus. They're even selling Mohammed teddy bears on eBay, for God's sake. This is not a good result for Islam. But then it so rarely is these days.

I was listening to a radio interview with a member of the Sudanese parliament, and he was asked if he was insulted by the Prophet's name being used like this, and he said: "No, the Prophet Mohammed is beyond any insult."

Well, isn't it just a shame that so many of his hare-brained followers are not.

But I guess that's what happens when little men get hold of big ideas they don't know how to handle.

Men who call themselves scholars and who think they're educated because they've memorised the Koran, which admittedly is quite an achievement, even if it has got nothing to do with knowledge or wisdom and everything to do with self-hypnosis.

But now that she's been pardoned and she's coming back to Britain, presumably things will start to return to normal. The Sudanese government will carry on murdering its own people while we stand by and watch.

We'll send money to help, of course, as usual, even if much of it does end up in private Swiss bank accounts, as usual.

And then we'll wait for the next bunch of opportunistic ignoramuses to disgrace their religion by choosing to be offended yet again about absolutely nothing at all.

It's so pathetic in a way that it's almost hardly worth generating the contempt, but I feel like making the effort, don't you?

Peace to all teddy bears, whatever they're called.

31

Pimping for Jesus

December 18, 2007

We've been following the American election campaign quite closely in the United Kingdom, mainly because our country has been acting like the fifty-first state for so long that he kind of feels like our president too now, God help us.

And of course we realise that this is a very important choice, not just for Americans, but for everybody on the planet. This is not the sort of job you can stroll into with your head up your ass hoping for a major atrocity to give you an excuse to attack a country that had nothing to do with it. That's not going to happen – any more.

I suppose it was inevitable that the Republican campaign would degenerate at some point into an unsavoury squabble about who is a bigger pimp for Jesus, because two of the candidates, Mr Huckabee and Mr Romney, have realised that the evangelical lobby is still there waiting for somebody it can call its own; still waiting for that special someone who will actually do something about the rapture.

So they've both decided to run on the 'theo-democracy' ticket. This is a new word, theo-democracy, which has been coined as a euphemism for what might be more honestly described as the Christian jackboot.

A society ruled by Christian values is what they want. Not the values of Christ. No, the values of Christians. Yes, I can almost hear that shiver running down your spine from here.

To this end, Mr Romney has been very keen to reach out to the evangelicals, but because he's a Mormon they're not sure they can trust him yet. They're thinking: "This guy might be crazy. Let's hope he is so we can vote for him."

He's a member of a bizarre sect that believes an angel turned up about 180 years ago with some gold plates, and as a result of this they all have to wear special underwear. I don't know whether that would be considered crazy enough, but if not, he also said recently that freedom requires religion, which I think pushes him way over the line, because freedom requires religion like a slug requires salt.

When you embrace religion you give up your freedom; that's the deal. You submit.

And it's why you need faith, because there's no rational reason for you to submit, so you have to talk yourself into it. That's what faith is.

Mormonism is not a high profile religion here in the UK. In fact I didn't even know about the special underwear until just this week. I suppose I've always regarded Mormons, I dunno, a bit like Jehovah's Witnesses. The kind of people who, when they knock on your door, you don't want to be rude, but you don't want to be polite either.

So when I first heard that there might actually be a Mormon president, I was a little surprised of course, but then I thought: Why not? America is a very egalitarian society. Why not a Mormon? Indeed, why not a Jehovah's Witness? What the hell, why not go all the way and elect a Scientologist? Anything but an atheist. Because atheists are the enemies of freedom, and a threat to the American way of life, according to Mr Romney.

In fact, I'm just wondering now how long it's going to be before somebody actually uses the phrase: "War on atheism", because I think you'd get quite quite a number of people signing up to that one in the name of religious freedom.

I get e-mails from people who live in the Bible Belt and who tell me they're afraid to go public as atheists because they think it would affect the family business if people knew they didn't believe in God. Is this the kind of religious freedom America is so proud of? Praise the Lord, or else?

And they always dress it up, too, in such a nice little package, as if Christianity equals patriotism. This is a peculiarly American idea. This is not something I've ever seen anywhere else, this notion that Christianity and patriotism are somehow connected, when the truth is American Christians are the last people that you would call patriotic, because they worship a foreign god.

I mean if you're going to worship a god, at least make it a North American one – there must be hundreds to choose from. Show a little loyalty to the land of your birth, people. No wonder you're losing the plot. Your religion has no roots. You're praising the wrong Lord.

Mind you, here in Europe we can't really criticise, because we're just as bad. I've always found it quite odd that we revere the ancient Greeks for their great discoveries in science and philosophy, and yet we dismiss their religion as fantasy, while embracing the religion of a culture that could barely rub two sticks together to make fire.

If only we had gone with the more civilised Greeks, who knows where we might be today? Actually we'd probably be be blaming Pandora for all our troubles on earth instead of Adam and Eve, and creationists would be forcing children to believe that the world came out of an egg laid by a giant black-winged bird. There but for Genesis, and the god of the desert, because that's the god we chose for ourselves, for reasons best known to ourselves.

And with this god there is no dialogue, hence there is no freedom, because with this god you obey or you perish. That's the arrangement. Submit or be damned. On your knees or be tortured forever you miserable sinner who'll never be worthy enough and whose soul will never be pure enough, but God loves you anyway, you worthless piece of crap.

Who wouldn't be seduced by such blandishments?

Who wouldn't want to prostrate themselves in humble gratitude?

Well me, actually, for one, thanks all the same. Because religion has had thousands of years to make a convincing case for itself, and yet this is the kind of thing it still has to resort to; crude coercion and childish threats of eternal punishment.

And as for all this talk about freedom and religion, the one thing we never hear about is freedom from religion, and I think this is the most important thing of all, because Mr Romney wouldn't even be a Mormon today if he hadn't been raised that way. He'd be wearing regular underpants like everybody else.

But he was brainwashed into it as a child. He was hypnotised into it as a child. And now, despite his obvious intelligence, he's clearly unable to shake it off, even though it's a hindrance to him in what he's now trying to achieve.

Far from being free, he's a slave to the childhood programming that keeps this mind virus alive generation after generation. And there's nothing he can do about it, even though he must know in his heart that this is the one thing that's likely to keep him out of the White House. Oh well, never mind. He'll always have Jesus.

Peace to everyone, especially to atheists, and other crazy un-American freedom-mongers.

32

Partying with Baby Jesus

December 24, 2007

Hi everyone. I've been asked by a number of people whether I celebrate Christmas. Well, of course I do. I celebrate every day I'm alive, quite frankly, and I find I'm particularly alive at Christmas.

So if your Christmas is anything like mine it will probably be a traditional family occasion of gluttony, drunkenness, long-held resentments bubbling to the surface, and fistfights over the dinner table. We usually book the ambulance for about six o'clock.

No, not really. Christmas is a time of peace and goodwill; everybody knows that. And it's also a time to celebrate the miraculous birth of Little Baby Jesus. And one thing Christmas has always done for me is it always reminds me that there are actually two separate versions of Jesus – the adult Jesus, obviously, with the beard and sandals who was murdered by the Jews, and Baby Jesus.

I've never connected those in my mind as being the same

person. They've always been completely separate entities to me. I never look at Baby Jesus in the crib and think: "Ah yes, I can see the resemblance." It wouldn't even occur to me (although it probably will now).

We actually have a little model Nativity scene in our house this Christmas, as we do every Christmas, ostensibly for the children, but really it's for everyone, because Christmas is for everyone.

Why do we have it? Well, for the same reason that we have a Christmas tree and fairy lights and tinsel and crackers and paper hats. Because it's fun.

To me, the Christmas story has always been a charming folk tale. I've never really connected it with religion in the sense that I've never associated it with sin or guilt or burning in eternal hellfire, which means I'm usually in a pretty good mood and ready to celebrate. But that doesn't mean I actually believe the story is true, any more than somebody who celebrates Halloween believes that witches really fly around on broomsticks, but it doesn't stop them from having fun with the idea.

Christmas was a folk festival long before Christianity ever got hold of it, and it will be long after Christianity's bony fingers have been prised off it, because newsflash for Christians – nailing your deity's name to a festival doesn't make it yours, I'm afraid. It's still all about the solstice. It's all about the rebirth of the sun. No, not the son of God, the regular sun.

It's a celebration of the life force, something that Christianity wouldn't really know very much about, because the only thing it celebrates is death.

All the supposed benefits of Christianity accrue after death, not before. Life is a penance to be endured, not lived – unless you're a televangelist with a million dollar mansion and a couple of Cadillacs, or a senior clergyman who happens to live in a palace, or two.

But the actual Nativity itself is an iconic scene which, of course, is instantly recognisable. A baby born in a stable, well that can only mean one thing. You never look at that scene and think to yourself: "I wonder if that's Baby Jesus there, or one of the many other babies known for being born in stables."

But, you know, it might not be a bad idea once in a while, because the Christmas story is by no means exclusive to Jesus. It was told and retold many times over the centuries long before Jesus was ever even thought of.

To the ancient Egyptians, Isis was the mother of God, and each midwinter they depicted her in a stable nursing a child that she had, guess what, miraculously conceived. And all this a couple of thousand years before Jesus. But there's no reason for that to spoil the party, because it's a folk tale, and they're meant to be reused and retold. It's all part of the magic. And, well, Christmas is a time for magic, and that's why, even though I don't believe in Santa Claus, I would never tell a child that there's no Santa Claus.

If I was going to tell them the blunt truth about anything I'd probably tell them that there's no Jesus – or if there is, his image rights have been hijacked by the forces of evil, and he now works directly for Satan, doing his best to keep us fearful and ignorant, making us feel less worthy than we really are, and emotionally crippling us with guilt for crimes that we had nothing to do with.

Doesn't that sound like the work of Satan?

Not that I really believe in Satan, by the way, I should emphasise that. But then we all know you don't actually have to believe in a thing for it to be a part of your life whether you like it or not, so in that sense I know he exists, and I also know the holy scriptures will back me up on that, which gives me a warm and fuzzy feeling all over, and isn't that really what Christmas is all about?

Well, that's enough from me. I want to wish everybody a merry Christmas, and I want to wish you what I wish for myself, which is of course peace, and may all your Christmases be godless and free.

33

Hook, Line and Rapture

January 8, 2008

Hi everyone. We all know that it doesn't have to make sense to make dollars and cents, and nobody knows this better than Mr Pat Robertson, the well-known televangelist, who for a while now has been broadcasting to Britain his familiar Christian message: Send us your money in Jesus' name.

With a personal fortune estimated at between two hundred million and one billion dollars, this guy wants you to send your money to help him do God's work. And no, he's not joking.

I understand that Mr Robertson doesn't particularly like to be called a televangelist, although when you consider some of the names he could be called I think he's getting away quite lightly with televangelist, don't you?

You may remember seeing him on television shortly after 9/11 agreeing with Jerry Falwell that the attack was caused by abortionists and lesbians, among others.

Or perhaps you saw him publicly urge the assassination of the

Venezuelan president, and although I'm sure we'd all agree that Mr Chavez has his faults, surely anyone that Pat Robertson wants dead can't be all bad.

But this is the kind of individual we're talking about, a real man of Christ, and a former Republican presidential candidate, too, as so many men of Christ seem to be these days.

But Mr Robertson is not just an ordinary religious wacko. To call him that would be to do him an injustice, because he's a very special kind of wacko.

Once a year he goes away to a prayer retreat where he talks to God, and yes, you've guessed it, God talks back to him.

Now there was a time when this kind of thing would have been regarded as schizophrenia. I dunno, I guess I'm just old fashioned that way. But this is what he does, he gets these messages from God which he then passes on to the lucky viewers of his television show. A bit like Moses coming down from the mountain, I suppose, because this guy obviously wants to be a prophet so bad, I wonder if he walks around at home dressed up in a bedsheet and talking Aramaic, maybe parting the waters in the bathtub occasionally just to keep in practice.

Last year's message from God was actually quite a serious one. It was a prediction by God that America would suffer a major atrocity in 2007, and he didn't mean that Fox News would be starting up a new channel.

No, it would be terrorism, but not intellectual terrorism.

And it might be nuclear. Or maybe even nucular, depending on your IQ.

Well, here we are in 2008 and of course we're all delighted

that nothing like this has happened. I guess the abortionists and lesbians just couldn't get their act together this time around.

But it does beg a rather important question, and that is: If God got this prediction wrong, does this mean that God is fallible, or is he a liar? Because either one would render him imperfect, which is of course impossible, so we're left to conclude, however uncomfortably, that it's Mr Robertson himself who is either lying or delusional, or maybe even both. Because, you see, I happen to know for a fact that God does not exist, because he came to me recently in a dream and told me so.

Oh yes. You believe in divine revelation, don't you? Because I certainly do, now.

Initially I was sceptical. Surprisingly, I even heard myself saying: "But God, if you don't exist, how come you're talking to me now?"

And he said: "This is a dream, you prick."

Well, I couldn't argue with that, obviously. So I said: "Fair enough, but do you think I could at least have it in writing?"

He said: "Yeah, why not? You can take this copy of the Bible."

I said: "What Bible? That's just a blank piece of paper."

He said: "This is the non-fiction version."

And this is a true story, by the way. I know some of you are going to be sceptical about this, but please let me assure you that this is absolutely true. Well, when I say it's true, it's not true in the literal sense, obviously, but it would be if it were, which is, I think, the most important thing.

It is true in another sense, in what we call the biblical sense. In other words it's fantastically improbable and impossible to verify, so naturally I intend to live my life henceforth in strict accordance with it to the detriment of everyone around me, and I'd like everyone to respect that.

I'd also like to preach this message high and low throughout the land to everyone who wants to hear it, and to everyone who doesn't. And I'd like to continue preaching it at them over and over again whether they like it or not.

I'd like to raise large amounts of revenue on the back of this activity, on which I would like to pay no tax.

I'd like to see my views forced into the educational curriculum, disproportionately represented in the law of the land, and displayed prominently outside every court house, if that's not too much trouble.

And if anyone would like to join my organisation, because it will be an organisation by this stage, it will only cost them ten percent of everything they earn for the rest of their life.

Praise the Lord, brothers and sisters, for he has revealed the truth to me, that he is a figment of our imagination, and furthermore that Christianity is nothing but a primitive death cult masquerading as a religion.

Everything about Christianity is stolen from earlier cultures, earlier belief systems. Nothing about it is real, except for its obsession with death. Christianity worships death as the ultimate sacrament. It revels in death. You might as well have death up there on the altar grinning down at you like a Halloween pumpkin, because that's what you're celebrating, not life. You could say that Christianity makes death worth living, which I think makes it the greatest con trick that's ever been perpetrated on mankind, and there have been a few.

And like all great cons, the sucker still thinks he's going to take the big prize even while he's standing there with his dick in his hand. Which is why there are Christians on this planet who have bought into this cult of death so completely that they actually want this world to end. They welcome things like global warming as a sign of approaching end times. Whenever there's a natural disaster they sing hallelujah. They literally can't wait to die.

And in the meantime, millionaire men of Christ like Mr Robertson will be on hand to pray for their gullible souls all the way to the bank. Everyone's a winner.

Peace, and a happy rapture to one and all.

34

O Dhimmi Canada

January 19, 2008

Well, once again free speech is under attack from a small group of Muslim fanatics, this time in Canada, where _Maclean's_ magazine is being hauled before a couple of laughably named "human rights commissions" for printing an article about the threat of militant Islam to our freedom in the West, and our bone-headed complacency in the face of it.

A group of law students saw an opportunity to be offended by this, because they've been waiting for just such an opportunity, of course, and they pounced on it like pigs on truffles

And they don't want justice here, because they know that justice would tell them to go and screw themselves. What they want is legal victory, a completely different thing. And they've got that before the case is even heard, because even if it's thrown out it will still incur great expense, for the defendants, for the magazine, not the plaintiffs – it will cost them precisely nothing.

And, if precedent is anything to go by, it will be decided, not on whether there was any truth in the article, but on whether anyone's precious feelings were hurt, or might have been hurt, and how certain members of the unelected commission feel about that.

This case is important to all of us in the West, because if this is tolerated it will start to happen everywhere. Newspapers and magazines that are even mildly critical of political Islam will be under pressure to censor themselves or face another expensive law suit, brought at no cost, and with the complacent connivance of a guilt-ridden patronising liberal establishment of self-haters and hand-wringers who are so ashamed of their own culture they can't stop apologising for it, and who, in doing so, give us every reason to be ashamed.

So what if a few fanatics are offended? It won't do them any harm. It will give them a idea of how the rest of us feel when we are confronted with cases like this.

On the other hand (and let's face it, there's always another hand, unless you're a Saudi Arabian shoplifter, of course) hurt feelings can be quite traumatic. I've heard that it can take seconds, sometimes even minutes, to get over it. So I'm not a bit surprised that Canadians are sympathetic, because they're a very warm and welcoming people, and I know this because I lived and worked there for several years.

So I also know that they're not fools, and they can see they're being taken for a ride here, that their well-meant humanitarian laws are being twisted and used against them by people to whom the very idea of human rights is blasphemy.

They can see that bringing this case is nothing but an act of legal terrorism, a lowdown dirty little stunt with no moral weight whatsoever, and that those who indulge it and who connive with it are not only making fools of themselves, they're making a fool of their country, when they'd be far better employed focussing on the genuine human rights of young girls shipped off to forced marriages, or murdered for refusing to go.

Do you want my opinion? No? Good. Here it is anyway.

I think this cynical stunt will backfire. Far from intimidating people into silence, I think this will encourage free speech and make those of us who care about it doubly determined to speak out.

Look what happened with the cartoons. The famous one with the turban bomb, that's all over the internet now, and it will always be all over the internet. It will never go away. If they hadn't made a fuss it would have been forgotten long ago.

Every incident like this will simply put a little more steel into people's resolve not to accommodate political Islam.

We already know in our hearts there's no reason why we should have to accommodate this repressive medieval ideology which most of us in the West frankly don't want anywhere near our society, and we should be entitled to say that openly and freely without fear of persecution.

Free speech is not negotiable. If we allow it to be compromised even slightly here they'll continue to chip away at it by whining and complaining and suing until they've worn it right down. You know they will, and so do they. And if we let that happen our children will never forgive us.

Some say that the western world is already well on its way to hell in a handbasket. Well, maybe not quite in a handbasket; we'll have to wait and see if we can stretch the budget that far after Halliburton and Blackwater have taken their cut. But we are on a slippery slope. Freedom is cheap to us now, because we're governed mainly by people of my generation who have never had to fight for the liberty they abuse in such a cavalier manner and take so much for granted.

They don't value it for themselves, because they don't know its true value, and they certainly don't value it for the likes of you and me.

So, if you're happy about that, and you're content for your freedom to be filtered through other people's narrow beliefs and prejudices, then you can roll over and go back to sleep now.

But if, like me, you're not happy about it and you hear somebody demanding special privileges based on their faith, then you're entitled to let them know exactly what you think about their demands. You've got as much right to be offended as they have.

The dhimmi human rights Stalinists will try to shut you up, of course, because free speech puts them out of a job. But if enough people speak out they can't drag us all in front of their poxy commissions, their preposterous toytown star chambers. They can't turn us all into criminals for having a free opinion in a free country.

It's utterly ridiculous that we should have to trip over other people's unprovable beliefs every time we turn around. We treat the religious with more consideration than we treat the disabled. How long before the women on these absurd commissions start wearing headscarves out of respect? It can only be a matter of time.

You know, I think ordinary Muslims in Canada who just want a peaceful life (as I know most of them do), I think they could argue that by taking on this bullshit case and giving it publicity it doesn't deserve, the human rights commissions have themselves unnecessarily increased tensions and resentment towards Muslims and perhaps even made it more likely that they'll be abused. And I think any Muslim who took that one on and who sued these unelected self-righteous nonentities right back into the cosy PC universe they live in would become an instant national hero. Ain't that the truth, O Canada? Peace, eh?

35

God the Psycho

February 2, 2008

I just had an e-mail from somebody who said: "I hope you find God in 2008", which is a very positive sentiment, and thank you very much for that. However, I hope you're wrong about it because from what I've heard about God and the way he likes to do things – particularly the kind of people he tends to attract – well, all these things have combined to make me hope he stays as far away from me as humanly, or inhumanly, possible.

We are talking, of course, about the god of the desert, the god of death. And we know that all three desert dogmas are variations on the same death cult, and they all worship this same god of supposed love and benevolent mercy, which is presumably why they hate each other with such a violent passion. I don't know, you'd have to ask them that.

Collectively they're known as the children of Abraham because Abraham is the original patriarch to whom they all trace themselves back. In fact, without Abraham's influence there's a chance that none of these dogmas would even exist today, which makes me wish there was some way that I could travel back in time and give him a severe talking to.

"You stupid idiot," I'd say. "Couldn't you foresee what would happen? Some prophet you turned out to be."

Abraham is the person who originally decided that there would only be one god from here on in. One size fits all, that was his message. And this would have had quite a devastating effect on the god community at the time. All the gods of the rivers and the mountains and the woods and so on – the local small specialised gods that had served people so well for generations – they would have found themselves squeezed out of the picture, or forcibly amalgamated into one giant elemental conglomerate with centralised control, a narrow moral code, and righteous vengeance in its heart.

Even to this day it's a matter of some conjecture whether this was the right direction for the human race to take at that particular time. The debate goes on.

Appropriately, given the religions he spawned, Abraham was not particularly noted for his mental stability. He was famously prepared to kill his own son because he heard God telling him to.

Fortunately, God intervened at the last second and stayed his hand, proving what a just and merciful god he is, if you ignore the severe psychological trauma he has just inflicted on these two unfortunate people. Scarred both of them for life, no question about that.

But that's pretty much par for the course, isn't it, for the Old Testament. Everyone ends up scarred mentally, physically.

Hardly anyone comes out in one piece.

Look at the treatment dished out to Adam and Eve, the very first people on the planet. They were punished for being true to their nature, the very nature that God endowed them with. He knew they were curious, he knew they had to be curious to survive, so he knew that they would eat the apple.

A cynical person might start to suspect that God only created us in the first place in order to punish us, because this is the first lesson we learn in Genesis – that being human is a sin. We were punished and driven from paradise for the sin of being true to our nature.

But we pulled ourselves together and we started on the Tower of Babel,* because we wanted to get up to heaven and have a look round. We were being curious, doing what comes naturally. But God didn't like that much either, so he punished us by destroying our language.

So here we are, we're barely a few pages into the Bible and already we've taken two massive body blows from our loving and merciful god.

Shortly after this he floods the entire planet because somebody must have looked at him the wrong way. He does tip off one person to build a boat, because obviously he doesn't want everybody wiped out, otherwise there'd be nobody left to punish.

Now I can understand somebody would read the Bible for pleasure because it's arguably a great work of literature; it's certainly an interesting cultural artifact, but it's not the word of

---

* Yes, I know I've placed the Tower of Babel and the Flood in the wrong order and that negates everything I've ever said. I take it all back. Praise the Lord.

God, and it's really time that we stopped pretending that it is, or even that it might be.

God is the main character in the book, and if you read it you'll quickly see this. He's an interesting personality, if a little crudely drawn. He's basically an attempt to put a human face on the creative life force, but unfortunately we've saddled him with all our petty prejudices and made him a bit too human for our own good. Because one thing I've noticed is that being human really only works for humans. It doesn't transfer at all well to deities. Human gods tend to be wilful, violent and unpredictable in a shallow ego-driven kind of way. The only thing boundless about them is their eagerness to take offence, like so many of the sensitive souls who worship them.

But if you're looking for offence, well then look no further than the Bible, surely one of the most offensive books that you could read, unless you believe that adulterers should be killed, or that it's OK to sell your daughter into slavery, or that anyone who works on the Sabbath should be stoned to death on the spot.

Maybe you're fine with all that. Or with the fact that God repeatedly advocates mass murder. Granted, he doesn't specifically mention cluster bombs and cruise missiles, but no doubt this is where the fine art of biblical interpretation comes in.

This guy's got a track record that would make Saddam look like Gandhi. In Deuteronomy 13, according to God, if you hear of a city where another god is worshipped you must kill everybody in that city; men, women, children, babies, even cattle. And then you must burn that city to the ground. Oh, and by the way, thou shalt not kill.

So I hope you can see why I have trouble embracing this god of the desert, this god of death that you seem to be so fond of, and I hope you can understand why I want nothing to do with him whether he exists or not. I simply don't share his values. I find them to be quite literally inhuman.

So I really don't care what he's got to say about anything, and if he came clumping down from heaven right now in a big pair of hobnail boots, waving the Book of Judges in my face, I'd simply tell him what I tell every other evangelising prick I meet: "No thanks, I'm not interested in your phoney salvation. I prefer damnation. Now piss off, I've got some sinning to do."

Peace, if that's not too blasphemous. Wouldn't want to hurt anybody's precious feelings.

36

Sharia Fiasco

February 10, 2008

Well, it seems that the Archbishop of Canterbury is shocked at the reaction to his verbal suicide bomb.* He received quite a lot of abuse. One person even called him a Judas, which I thought was a little unfair. What did Judas ever do to deserve that kind of abuse? Yes, OK, he betrayed Jesus, but the Christian Church has betrayed him every day for the last two thousand years, and nobody seems to care about that.

The Archbishop is a very clever man, but he's clever in a useless way, because he lives in a bubble. All this stuff is theoretical to him. None of it will impact on his life in any way, so he can well afford to be magnanimous about it.

Personally, I don't think it will affect his credibility, because I don't think he ever had any in the first place, but I think his words are important because they're symptomatic of a wider malaise in British society.

* He said it was inevitable that Britain would have to accommodate sharia.

Whenever there's a clash between Islamic culture and the indigenous culture here in Britain (yes, I did use the word indigenous, as opposed to Islamic, i.e. alien and foreign – just thought I'd clear that one up), whenever they clash, the indigenous culture is always presumed to be in the wrong, in the interests of community cohesion, of course.

For example, polygamy is illegal in Britain, but Muslim polygamists not only get away with it, they now also receive extra state benefits for their extra wives.

Hate speech is banned in Britain, for everyone except extremist Muslim imams, who are free to preach hatred against Jews and homosexuals because if we required them to obey the law they might be offended.

I would say that we ought to be ashamed of ourselves, but of course we already are, which is why all this is happening.

Western society has its faults, as we all know, and as the Islamists themselves never tire of pointing out, but personally speaking they're faults that I can live with. Islam on the other hand has faults that I can't live with and I won't live with under any circumstances, and a lot of people in this country feel exactly the same way.

The reason that we don't want any aspect of sharia law in our society is because it's a manifestation of clerical fascism, and because it favours men over women, which makes it a violation of civilised democratic values. And the reaction that the Archbishop received, which obviously did affect him (which just goes to show what a bubble he really does live in, and it also explains why so many Muslims were puzzled by his remarks), but the reaction is an illustration of the anger that people feel at not being allowed to express an honest opinion about Islam in our society, because rather than calling things honestly by their name, we're always encouraged to hide behind cowardly euphemisms to avoid offending people who've got nothing to be offended about.

Just last week, for example, we were issued with special politically correct guidelines about how we should refer to Islamic terrorism lest we give the false impression that it's got anything to do with Islam. We're talking about terrorism carried out in the name of Islam, by Muslims, and justified using their holy scripture. But apparently it's got nothing to do with Islam. Well, I'm sorry, but just because every Muslim doesn't support it doesn't mean it's not Islamic.

People say you can't judge Islam by its followers, but that's like saying you can't judge a football team by its results. Islam is its followers. Because there's no central authority the Koran is open to interpretation by men who, being human, will always interpret to suit their own cultural prejudices. So Islam is its followers. It's a representation of how they interpret their holy book, and therefore the only way it can be judged is by their behaviour.

Unfortunately right now for all of us (that's Muslims and non-Muslims alike) the driving force behind the religion is Saudi Arabia, where most of the terrorist money comes from, and where many of the so-called community leaders in Britain get their funding. And this particular brand of Islam preaches intolerance, hatred, and righteous bloodlust to children.

And people like the Archbishop, who think that every situation can be resolved by respectful dialogue even while the people they're talking to are stepping on their faces, these people are part of the problem, not the solution.

The solution is not more appeasement, dialogue and debate. The solution is to enforce the law equally and impartially for everyone, regardless of whether it's inconvenient for some Muslims. The solution is to prosecute those who incite terror, to close down the mosques and deport the imams. Any sane society would be doing this automatically.

We need to stop treating Islam like a special needs case. If I were a Muslim I'd be insulted by it. The police should stop consulting with these so-called community leaders before raiding premises or making arrests. They should stop pussyfooting around in mosques. If a criminal is hiding there, go in and get him out.

There should be no more pandering to Muslim sensibilities in the public arena. No footbaths in public washrooms, no separate days for swimming where nobody else is allowed, no special job conditions that don't apply to others, and nobody should be allowed to teach children or appear in court while wearing a ridiculous mask.

There should be no restrictions on non-Muslims, like when Scottish Health Service staff were forbidden to eat lunch at their desks during Ramadan in case somebody happened to be fasting nearby. And there should be no cultural sensitivity of any kind involving Christmas or pigs or dogs.

In fact, just a couple of weeks ago the classic children's story of the Three Little Pigs was censored by a committee of English middle class bedwetters desperate to show how culturally sensitive they are at everybody else's expense.

And it's a classic story. We all know the story, I'm sure. The three little pigs, they're building their houses, one of brick, one of wood, and with a naivete that would embarrass even a dhimmi Archbishop, one of straw.

And we all know what happens. The big bad wolf comes along and blows down the first two houses, but he can't blow down the brick one, so he flies an airplane into it and blames the Jews.

Isn't that it? No? Gosh, you know it's so long since I read the story, I guess I'll have to go back and read it again, that's if I can find a copy that hasn't been pulped in the interests of community cohesion.

Peace to everyone, especially to all those Muslims who are as embarrassed as I am by this cloistered bubble-headed fool of an Archbishop.

37

Take a Cruise, Tom

February 22, 2008

One religion, if you'll pardon the expression, which has been in the news lately is Scientology, which I have to say I don't know very much about. It's not nearly as high profile here in Britain as it is in America. I don't think any celebrities are involved, at least not yet.

From what I can gather it was founded by a science fiction writer, which might help to explain why they believe that human beings are burdened by entities who are part of the fallout from some ancient intergalactic genocide, and that practising Scientology is a way to rid yourself of the influence of these entities.

So pretty much your standard religious bullshit, then. You're contaminated and need to be cleansed by experts, for a price. The original sin common to most religions, it seems. There's something wrong with being human. Well, well, who would have thought it?

Some people consider Scientology to be a sinister cult, and, well, even if it is, we've never had a problem with sinister cults in the past. We've positively nurtured them and allowed them to grow into the monstrous dogmas that currently plague every aspect of life on this planet, so why are we so upset about this particular bunch of lunatics?

And shouldn't people have a choice? Let's say you've got a taste for religious insanity, but not the mainstream kind, and you're casting around for something a little different, because you don't want to follow the crowd. What are you, a sheep? Of course not. Now you've got a cool alternative. You've got your Scientology.

And although people do talk about it in a negative terms, it does have positive aspects which I think we should acknowledge. For example, they haven't initiated any mass suicides or mass murders as far as I'm aware, and I think that's a very positive thing.

However, as with all fanatical religious cults, it does have its negative side. For example, they're notoriously litigious by all accounts, which means they probably do have something to hide. And they also have a reputation for harassing people who criticise them, which is very negative if it's true, and I'm not saying it is – not yet, anyway.

Also, I have to say that if a member of my family were to join any organisation that urged them to reject their family and friends and turn their back on the life they knew, I'd say that would be a very negative thing. And I think anyone prepared to do something that unnatural would be operating under a powerful negative influence.

However, having said all this, I still find myself attracted to Scientology because it ends in "...ology", and it contains most of the word "science", which gives it a vague air of authority to gullible uneducated people like myself.

And if you want to know the secrets you have to join the gang. I mean, what would it cost me anyway? A few hundred, a few thousand? OK, maybe a few hundred thousand, plus my sanity, but everything in life has risks.

I'm certainly not worried about being brainwashed. Are you kidding? I'm a Catholic. I've been done. I've been through the full rinse cycle. Fluff dried, ironed and folded. So don't talk to me about being brainwashed.

So yes, I'm keen to find out more about this religion, but unfortunately there is one small obstacle, and that is the poster boy himself, Mr Tom Cruise. I just have such a serious problem with his movies, because he always seems to be playing somebody who's taller than he really is, and this just doesn't work for me. In the back of my mind I'm thinking: "This guy's acting tall. Why is he pretending? What is he ashamed of?"

Being small is fine. There's nothing wrong with being small. I know lots of small people, and they're all wonderful.

If Tom Cruise played small movie heroes it would do small people's image a lot of good on this planet, but no, instead he chooses to perpetuate the illusion and reinforce the stereotype that tall is good and small is bad.

If he's capable of this kind of moral dishonesty in observable life, what's he going to be like when it comes to the mysteries of life?

And if he's literally not prepared to stand up for the little guy, I have to ask myself: Is this the kind of person I want to be associated with, and how much can his religion really offer me?

So yes, although I'd like to find out more about Scientology, I'm afraid this guy is just in the way, and I really don't see a way past this.

If he were to jump into a little space pod and disappear off this planet to pastures new, taking his ridiculous movies with him of course, well then I might be inclined to examine Scientology a bit more closely, but until then I'm afraid it will have to remain a big fat mystery to me. Oh well, you can't win them all. Nanu nanu.

38

Appeasing Islam

March 8, 2008

According to a recent opinion poll many Muslims say that the way for the West to have better relations with Islam is to show it more respect. And who said Muslims don't have a sense of humour?

Given that Islam is officially above criticism in the West, it's hard to imagine how we could give it any more respect short of closing down all the pubs, growing beards, and beating up women who don't want to dress like nuns…

Ah yes, of course. Silly me.

I think many people in the West are now realising that Islam has already been given far too much respect, especially here in Europe, where according to another poll, people now see it as a threat to their culture.

They carry on accommodating its every demand of course, but this not because Islam is welcome in Europe – far from it. It's because people have been conditioned by the lie of multiculturalism to believe that what they should think is more important than what they do think.

So, although people will criticise Islam in private, they know that to do so publicly, in other words to be honest about their feelings, would instantly make them racists and Islamophobes and Nazis and disgusting imperialist ethnocentric fascist bastards grinding their jackboots into the faces of the innocent and the weak. So best not make a fuss. You want to beat your wife and mutilate your daughter? Be our guest. We'll even subsidise it, because we want to be your friend. What's that? You want to destroy our corrupt society? Well, that's our fault, not yours. Here, have some more money.

This film* that's coming out in Holland shortly which has got the whole country in a state of heightened terrorist alert is yet more proof that everything in Europe now needs to be measured against the possibility of Muslim violence. Every play, every film, every art exhibition, every magazine article – in fact our whole culture is now subject to Muslim approval.

But then this is Europe, and we have a history of appeasement and caving in to threats. Radical Islam knows this, and is playing us like a violin. They know that Islam will never get blamed for anything in Europe, no matter what happens. So that, for example, when the Danish press reprinted the cartoons recently, which was followed by a week of rioting by Muslim youths, Copenhagen's chief of police refused to admit that it had anything to do with the cartoons. He said it was because they

* Geert Wilders' film *Fitna*.

were bored. Yes, that's right, they all rushed out and set fire to the city every night for a week for something to do. If only they'd had a table tennis club.

The whole thing happened because three Islamic fanatics were caught planning to murder the cartoonist. Imagine how bored they must have been.

Oh yes, also, a newsflash for European journalists. An anti-Semitic attack by Muslims on Jews is not a conflict between communities. In case you hadn't noticed, Islam hates Jews. Even if Israel didn't exist Islam would still hate Jews. Their holy book tells Muslims that they should hate Jews.

So I think you'll find what's happening is not a conflict between communities at all, but a violent unprovoked racist attack by Muslims on Jews, because they're Jews. Just thought I'd clear that one up for you so that you can report it accurately next time, if you bother to report it at all.

If we were serious about respecting Islam we would give it an honest reality check. Islam needs to adapt to Europe, not the other way round. I know a lot of Muslims agree with this and they make the effort to adapt and to rub along with everybody else, which is great and it's very welcome, but we all know that a lot of others don't, which is why many European cities have large Muslim ghettos controlled by religious bigots where indigenous laws and values are increasingly unwelcome; places full of people who have no intention of integrating and who want nothing less than the end of our civilisation, while we pander and defer to them thanks to a biased press, a complacent judiciary, and the kind of politicians you wouldn't wish on your worst enemy. Actually, you probably would.

And this situation is as much a threat to the freedom of ordinary Muslims as it is to everybody else. And it's a clear indication that what we need in Europe now is not more respect for Islam. It's less respect for Islam, and more respect for ourselves.

We need to stop pretending (because that's what we're doing pretending) that all cultures are equal, when we can clearly see that they're not.

Islamic culture is not equal to western culture. It encourages violence against women, against Jews and homosexuals. It sanctions polygamy and marrying old men to young children in a disgusting travesty of human relations. Anyone in the West advocating these kinds of values would very quickly find themselves in jail.

It's not equal. It's inferior. And given radical Islam's openness about its totalitarian agenda, this is not something that should be encouraged in any way. It should be discouraged by firm legislation, and by rigorous enforcement of the law. Remember the law?

Now I know that I'm going to be accused of racism and Islamophobia by the usual self-righteous pinheads, but I don't mind, because those words have no value in this context. One has been neutralised by repeated dishonest misuse, and the other is just a barefaced lie concocted by the political left in tandem with the religious right in a marriage of convenience which is quite simply beneath contempt.

A phobia is an irrational fear. Resisting Islam is not irrational. Pandering to it is irrational. Indulging the lie that Islamic culture is somehow equal to western culture while ignoring the victims of that culture is more than irrational. It's downright criminal.

And if you really want to talk about racism, then look no further than the poisonous fiction of multiculturalism, a divisive and patronising racist ideology.

And the governments of Europe who promote it are racist governments. The civil servants who pander to it are racists. The university lecturers who encourage it are racists. The journalists who lie about it are racists. And the ordinary people who say one thing in private and another in public are cowardly racist hypocrites.

If we can't bring ourselves to say what's in our hearts when it truly matters then we've already given up our freedom, and with it the freedom of future generations, which is something that we've got no right to do.

We didn't earn this freedom. It was handed to us on a plate by people who did earn it with their lives. We don't own it. We're custodians of it. It's not ours to give away.

So it's time to speak up, Europe. It's time to stop whining and bellyaching about the Americans for five minutes and show a little backbone for once, just once.

Or do we want to spend the rest of our lives cowering like frightened mice from a handful of violent bigots who think they have a right to poke a finger into our chest and tell us how we're allowed to live, what we can and can't do, say and think?

Well, I don't know about you, but anyone who asks me that question is going to get a very short answer, and I'll give you a clue, it won't contain the words "Allah" or "akbar".

Peace. Wouldn't that be nice?

39

The Religion of Fear

March 31, 2008

Hi everyone. Well, now that the *Fitna* furore has died down somewhat it's interesting to see how many people are condemning the film, and how few people are condemning the thuggish intimidation that forced LiveLeak* to remove it.

What happened to all those people who keep telling us: "I don't agree with what you say, but I'll defend your right to say it?"

Where have they all gone? Maybe they're on vacation.

No shortage of politicians, however, lining up to accuse the film of falsely equating Islam with violence, which is a bit like falsely equating Walt Disney with Mickey Mouse.

I'm sure anyone who follows the news would also equate Islam with violence. I know I certainly do, because any time anybody criticises Islam they're usually threatened with violence. Islam

---

* LiveLeak was the only video website brave enough to host the film. Death threats towards their staff forced them to remove it temporarily while security was improved, but they subsequently reinstated it. As far as I know, you can still see the film on the LiveLeak site.

without violence is like an egg-free omelette. The religion is predicated on violence and the threat of violence. It's a religion of peace in the same way that North Korea is a people's democratic republic. But we're not allowed to say that, because if we do we'll be threatened with violence.

When the film was actually removed, under threat of violence, some Muslims actually had the nerve to congratulate LiveLeak for promoting tolerance on the internet. I tell you, whenever I think about this stuff now I feel like I'm in a hall of mirrors, don't you?

To be fair, Dutch Muslims do deserve some praise, because they could have reacted violently and probably got away with it, we all know that, so all credit to them for not exploiting the situation. But the very fact that we are grateful to them pretty much proves the point of the film, because let's be clear about this, it was the threat of Muslim violence that caused the Dutch government to grovel in such abject dhimmitude and to run around apologising like headless chickens before and after the event, a spectacle which I'm sure many Muslims enjoyed, and why shouldn't they enjoy it? After all, it sends out a clear message to the entire Muslim world that in Europe we won't stand up for what we believe in (or what we say we believe in) and we will be intimidated into silence. All you've got to do is shake your fist, and we'll do exactly as we're told.

So Islam in Europe now enjoys the best of all possible worlds. It's a religion when it wants to be, it's a culture when it wants to be, and it's a race when it wants to be. It gets full rights on all three counts, demanding and getting respect wherever it goes, while giving absolutely none.

Hence we were treated recently to the spectacle of the Swiss foreign minister degrading herself and her country by putting on a headscarf before she was allowed to meet the homicidal leadership of Iran, in a cheap betrayal of all the brave women who have been murdered by these violent criminals in the name of Islam.

The Iranian government were among the first to criticise the film, too, taking time out from executing children, again in the name of Islam, to denounce it roundly. But I'm sure most people realise that this fake outrage is in no way genuine. It's all part of a cynical campaign of intimidation by the Islamic world to force unwanted Islamic values into western society.

And that's why in every free country there are now aggressive Islamist pressure groups, usually funded by the Saudis, who claim to speak for all Muslims, but who actually speak only for a small band of fanatical bigots like themselves, and who are very quick to insult our culture and our values as degenerate and immoral, while being themselves ultra sensitive to any perceived criticism, portraying themselves as victims, as oppressed, rather than the oppressors they are, knowing that if you repeat the lie often enough people will start to believe it. Mr Goebbels taught us that little nugget of wisdom, and the would-be authors of the next Holocaust have learned the lesson well.

Luckily for me I don't get insulted easily on a personal level, not even at being called a racist kuffar, as some idiot called me recently, but when somebody attacks my culture, well, that's a little different because that's an assault on my values. It diminishes my sense of self-worth, I believe it violates my human rights and I think it should be prosecuted as a hate crime. It's irrational, it's paranoid, and really I think there's only one word to describe it, and that is civilisationphobia. This is a word I like to use as a kind of umbrella word for a host of different phobias that manifest themselves in Islam, including:

Eleutherophobia – Fear of freedom.

Epistemophobia – Fear of knowledge.

Prosophobia – Fear of progress.

Peccatophobia – Fear of sinning, or imaginary crime.

Catagelophobia – Fear of being ridiculed.

Cenophobia – Fear of new things and ideas.

Cherophobia – Fear of gaiety (big fear of gaiety).

And the biggest fear of all, of course:

Gynophobia – Fear of women.

Islam is terrified of women, and that's why all over the internet you'll find clips from Arab television where, along with all the rampant Jew-hating and other propaganda aimed at turning children into murderers, you'll find clerics calmly explaining under what circumstances a man may beat his wife in the religion of peace. That's right, a man may beat his wife. And they wonder why we don't want this stuff in Europe.

If you lay a violent hand on a woman you're not a man, you're an animal, and I don't care how many so-called scholars tell you that cowardly brutality is the will of God. Chances are you've never been on the receiving end of the kind of punishment you like to dish out so freely. So I hope the Hindus have it right, because, if there's any justice, you will be reincarnated as a female homosexual Jew, and then you'll find out what a pain it is having to deal with violent primitive dickheads like you.

You know, when I was growing up I never thought I'd be ashamed to live in the twenty-first century. I thought it was going to be a new golden age, the space age, an age of knowledge and discovery. We'd have shaken off the shackles of superstition by now, surely. We'd have the technology to reach for the stars, maybe even create paradise right here on earth. I remember looking forward to it.

Well, here we are, and what have we got? We've got Islam, a violent seventh-century desert dogma that wants to take over the world, remove our freedom, subjugate women, brainwash children, persecute Jews and homosexuals, and drag us all back a thousand years. And all we can do is make excuses for it, for fear of causing offence. We really are pathetic, aren't we?

I think people living five hundred years from now will look back on this period of history and they'll laugh at us. Well, wouldn't you?

Peace.

40

The Curse of Faith

April 25, 2008

Hi everyone. First of all, can I just say to all the people who keep writing to tell me that I'm wrong when I say that Christians are born in debt to Jesus and don't I realise that that debt has already been repaid by Jesus? Well yes, of course. But only in the same way that a finance company will pay off all your current debts, but then you have to pay back the finance company, or there's going to be trouble.

Similarly, if you decide to welsh on the debt that you owe Jesus, the one he paid with his precious blood, then you're going to be in big trouble, my friend. In fact, big is probably too small a word to describe the kind of trouble you're going to find yourself in if you reject him as your saviour, because you're going to fry for eternity. And eternity is not to be trifled with, because it's forever. And we know this because they measured eternity and it came up exactly forever. And that's what's in store for you. Eternal unimaginable suffering, and Jesus isn't going to do a damn thing about it. Why? Because he doesn't give a shit. That's how much he loves you.

I think after two thousand years, if anything, he owes us another crucifixion. You can't live on past glories forever. Who does he think he is, Woody Allen? Come on.

Anyway, because of this, today I'd like to say a few words about faith, which I think has the potential to enslave us all by stealth, because I think faith is a very dangerous and misleading word. It contains two completely separate entities which have got nothing at all to do with each other. One is good, and one is evil. One is called spirituality and the other is called religion. One is a private experience, the other is a public nuisance. One leads to self-knowledge, the other to self-indulgence at everyone else's expense. In one there is no compulsion, whereas the other depends on compulsion for its survival. One is grounded in innocence, the other in guilt. One embraces life, the other worships death.

It's hard to imagine how these two things could be any more different. Yet for some reason they're always sold to us together in a single package under the banner of faith. If you take one, you've got to take the other. A bit like a pet shop giving away a free rattlesnake with every bunny rabbit.

I'm not saying there isn't more to this life than meets the eye, because there obviously is. Science has already shown us that. In the subatomic world it turns out that nothing is solid, if you can understand that, and some particles are so unpredictable we're not even sure if they exist or not. They seem to be there and not be there at the same − a bit like western democracy, or is that just me? But anyway, it's clear that we are part of a reality that we don't fully understand.

And if there is a life force in this universe (and let's face it there must be, otherwise there wouldn't be any life) it's natural that we would want to make some connection with it, because everybody wants to feel more alive, right?

But there's no evidence that it requires worshipping or any form of subservient behaviour, or that we are in any way central to its agenda, or even relevant to it, any more than any other organism on the planet, or in the universe – this universe or any other universe. So in that sense I think we really need to get over ourselves big time.

Also, we need to stop pretending that all the manmade trappings of faith, the ornamental accessories if you like, are really anything more than just that. I'm talking about scripture, dogma, ritual, prophecy, religious law. All these things that have been put there to give religion some kind of structure, and, to be fair, that's why they're there, isn't it?

It's a bit like dressing the invisible man. Once he's got some clothes on, you can see him. But of course you don't see him, you see the clothes. And that's the problem. Everyone's become so obsessed with the goddam clothes we've forgotten if there was ever anyone there in the first place.

If you're a spiritual person you don't need religion, and you know it. And you're certainly not interested in forcing your beliefs on to anybody else.

If you're not a spiritual person then what the bloody hell are you doing on your knees praying like an idiot? Like some dog that's been taught how to do something without understanding why. Get up and stop making a fool of yourself, because your faith is not a virtue, it's a vice. It's a slave to dogma, to scriptural certainties which are nevertheless open to self-interested interpretation by men. Now I'm sure even you can see the obvious flaw in that little arrangement.

Also, faith, in its Alice in Wonderland way, defines and measures itself according to lack of evidence. The less there is, the more faith is required, and the more worthy it is of respect and deference, for some reason. Not to mention large amounts of public money, generous tax breaks, and the freedom to fill the minds of innocent young children with violent superstitions and baseless fears.

And this, to me, really is the curse of faith, and it's something that shames us all from generation to generation. It's the cowardly way that we allow religion to be forced on to children in a clear violation of their human rights, hypnotising them almost at birth, hijacking their lives and turning them into little Christians, little Muslims, little Jews, before they have a chance to understand the first thing that's involved.

We live in such civilised times in the twenty-first century, don't we? Human rights are everything to us. We fall over ourselves to give compensation to every cheap chancer, every lowlife criminal scumbag whose precious feelings have been hurt, but we don't give a damn about the rights of children having their minds moulded and stunted by others before they've had a chance to fully form, like dead-heading flowers before they've bloomed. It's a crime against humanity, is what it is, and one day it will be against the law.

Tell that to Jesus, if you see him, and tell him from me to go and screw himself, to the nearest tree.

Peace, and who knows, maybe one day civilisation.

41

God Is Not Enough

May 23, 2008

Hi everyone. A lot of people seem to think that I've got something in particular against religion, but the truth is I would take exactly the same attitude towards any evil life-denying crackpot ideology.

Show me another dangerous death-embracing crock of supernatural bullshit and I would give it exactly the same treatment, I promise.

It's just that I believe religion is God's way of telling us that he doesn't exist.

And people often say to me: "What if you're wrong about that and God does exist, and you have to face him on Judgment Day? What will you say for yourself then, bigmouth?"

Well, what can I say? If that happens I'm screwed, aren't I? Let's be honest. I'm damned for all eternity. I'm going straight to hell. I know I can't expect any mercy, because we all know what a nasty piece of work he is. And it's unlikely that I'll be able to talk my way out of it, because God isn't stupid, unfortunately.

He's many other things, including petulant, callous, vindictive, spiteful, heartless, petty, cruel, and egotistical to a fault, but not stupid. So that's me down the chute, no question.

But if by some miracle I did manage to get in a word before the trapdoor opened, I'd probably ask God what kind of third rate operation he thinks he's running here on earth, and why he allows himself to be represented almost exclusively by gangsters, perverts and frauds into whose care you'd be as well advised to entrust your soul as you would your children.

I'd also remind God that six thousand years ago he threw us out of paradise for obtaining the knowledge of good and evil. So why don't we have it? We paid the price. Every child is born guilty. I couldn't imagine a higher price than that, could you? Yet we still don't quite seem to know the difference. Maybe the people of Burma could help us out with that.

But I wonder what went wrong. Was the fruit of the tree of knowledge faulty in some way, or is this just a straightforward case of out-and-out fraud?

Either way, I'll be demanding from God retrospective reinstatement in paradise for the entire human race, along with six thousand years of backdated blessings and a full apology. Well, why not? What have I got to lose? I'm already going to hell.

I expect I'll end up in Catholic hell, which I understand is a large black hole of guilt at the end of the universe from which nothing escapes, not even light – mainly because no light has ever got in, although apparently anything passing by too closely is liable to be sucked in and baptised.

But just because I believe that religion is a cynical perversion of the human spirit that exists purely for the benefit of the parasites that we know as clergy doesn't mean that I'm not looking for answers to the big questions just like anybody else.

You know, the questions that religion pretends it has answers to because it knows that for some people any answer is better than no answer at all.

Questions like: Why are we here? Where do we come from? Where are we going? – that sort of thing. Is there an afterlife, and if so, is it fully licenced for alcoholic drinks?

That last bit may seem like a trivial concern to you, but not to me, because I live in a society where many people enjoy a social drink from time to time. Not a huge amount, just enough to kill a horse. And in these enlightened days of the twenty-first century where everyone's human rights and cultural identity are so very important, I don't see why I should have to abandon my culture just because I'm dead. It's only the afterlife, not Saudi Arabia. Let's keep things in perspective.

Of course in reality we all know that there will be beer in heaven, and lots of it, otherwise it wouldn't be heaven, would it? It's almost not even worth pointing that out, but I thought I would anyway just in case somebody wants to take the opportunity to be offended.

People say to me: "You just don't understand the joy that a believer feels when they give their heart to God. You just don't get it."

Well, maybe that's true. But I do understand the desire for such a joyful heart, and I've got no problem with anyone who seeks it. I wish them well.

I can even understand how this joyful feeling could easily lead to a perfectly natural urge to share it with, and even, dare I say, impose it on others for their own spiritual good. And that I do have a problem with, as you probably know.

However, it occurred to me that I've been alive on this planet now for over half a century, and I still haven't got a clue what I'm supposed to be doing here. And frankly, yes, I am beginning to find that a little embarrassing. So I'm open to offers, broadly speaking, on the meaning of life. But a word of warning, it's going to have to be something that I can reasonably talk myself into without too much embarrassment, which means it's going to have to be fairly plausible, unfortunately, because that pretty much eliminates all religion, especially our three old friends the desert dogmas. I couldn't possibly have anything to do with them. Partly because I don't want to belong to a death cult, obviously. But also, I'd just like to find something with more of a spiritual dimension, like, I don't know, morris dancing perhaps, cheese rolling; I'm sure something will turn up.

It might actually help if I could narrow it down in advance and decide what kind of believer I would like to be – maybe that would help. You know, in broad terms. Would I like to be, say, open-minded, compassionate, joyful, optimistic, flexible, tolerant and wise? Or would I prefer to be closed-minded, bigoted, intolerant, dogmatic, gloomy, judgmental and censorious?

That's quite a difficult one. I can actually see both points of view there. Obviously if I go with the first option I'd be very popular, have a lot of friends, and everything would be great.

But if I go with the second one, people would quite rightly

despise me, but I'd then be able to claim persecution and maybe even get a couple of laws changed in my favour. Hmm. I think I'll give that one a little more thought.

In the meantime I'll keep looking, of course. I'll try to keep an open mind, because I think it's important to keep an open mind, and you won't convince me otherwise no matter what you say, so don't even try.

I'm not too fussy about what I end up believing in, as long as it's the truth. Or, if not, at least something that doesn't make me want to laugh out loud with derision whenever I think about it. In fact, the way things are going I'll probably settle for that. Peace, and a happy springtime to one and all.

42

A Secular World Is a Sane World

June 27, 2008

You know, a lot of people say to me: "I agree with you about Islam, but not about religion."

Well, thanks, but if that's the case you don't agree with me, because Islam is not the problem. Religion is the problem.

The allowances that we make for faith, and the respect that we give to belief without evidence, has encouraged Islam to push its way into a society where it really doesn't belong and threaten all our freedom.

But that's not Islam's fault. Its stated goal is to take over the world. It's just being true to itself. It's our fault for indulging religion in the first place, and for giving religious opinion a status in our society that it hasn't earned and doesn't deserve. Why? You tell me.

Animals don't seem to need gods in their lives, do they? Perhaps because they haven't got quite such a low opinion of themselves as we've been taught to have. Insignificant, unclean, in need of salvation. Recognise yourself?

If you're wretched enough to buy into that life-sucking drivel the only thing you need to be saved from is your own gullibility.

Your soul doesn't need cleansing, because it isn't dirty. And anyone who tells you different is telling you for their benefit, and not for yours, because the purpose of religion is the employment and the empowerment of clergy. That's its only purpose. You don't matter. You've never mattered. You don't seriously think any of those old frauds in the Vatican really believe in God, do you? Come on. God is for the little people. People like you and me. It's all about the clergy, who do very well out of it. How well? Let's ask the Archbishop of Canterbury, if we can find out which one of his two palaces he's currently staying in, and of course if he isn't too busy praying towards Mecca.

His recent disgraceful attempt to crowbar sharia law into British life is a good example of how some Christian clergy are so unprincipled they'll happily hitch their wagon to the crescent moon, to a religion they despise as heretical, in order to help push unwanted religious values into society at large, because for them any religious values are better than none.

The real enemy for both these dogmas is secularism, and that's what they're most afraid of, because they know it could threaten the generous tax breaks and the countless millions in public subsidy they're currently rolling around in. And that's why whenever you hear a speech from a religious leader nowadays it usually contains a warning against the danger of secularism.

When the Pope went to America recently it was the first thing he said when he got off the plane. Obviously he also apologised for all the child abuse, but what else was he supposed to say? Get over it you pussies? Of course not. Not even if he was thinking it, which he probably was. Oh come on, you know he was.

But secularism is not atheism, as many of these god-peddling faith jockeys will often try to pretend in order to frighten people who think they're going to be possessed by demons if society isn't run by God, or rather by men who think they're God.

There are plenty of religious people who are secularists. They believe in God, but they've got too much class to try and force their views on anyone else. And that's all secularism means. It means religious freedom for everybody, not just for religious people. It means respecting everyone's right to worship freely, but removing the power of the middleman, the clergyman, the self-appointed intermediary, to interfere and meddle uninvited in people's lives.

No wonder these pious parasites are more afraid of it than they are of hellfire itself. Seculophobia. Is that even a word? Well, I guess it is now.

I realise this all sounds very negative, but let me assure you that I'm actually very optimistic about the future of humanity, at least in the long term, because I just don't think it's possible for us to stay this stupid forever. We'll try, of course, and some of us will really dig our heels in too, no doubt, but I think despite ourselves we will eventually evolve into something a bit more intelligent, a bit more compassionate and a bit less afraid of our own shadow, and when that happens religion will simply die a natural death of acute embarrassment, if there's any justice.

The thing is, though, I don't want it to take thousands of years. I want it to happen now, partly because I'm a modern kind of guy and I want everything now, but also because it pretty much needs to happen now if we want to keep our freedom. If we don't shake off religion we are not going to shake off Islam. It's that simple, because Islam is here to stay. Any population projection will confirm that.

In a couple of generations some parts of Europe will have no choice but to democratically allow sharia law, which, as we know, discriminates against and victimises women, Jews, homosexuals, and pretty much anybody who isn't a heterosexual Muslim male, preferably with a beard.

So Islam needs to be neutralised in Europe, now before it's too late. Not by engaging it in respectful dialogue and throwing money at it as usual, but by doing what we should have done years ago and legistlating religion out of public life and back into the private domain where it belongs.

Right now Islam is laughing at us. It's watching us lead ourselves by the nose into submission. What can we do? Well, all any of us can do is speak out, while we're still allowed to. Because some Muslims are now demanding that criticising their religion be made a criminal offence. I suppose we should have seen that one coming really, shouldn't we?

It actually is a criminal offence in the Netherlands, it seems, where anyone satirising Islam is liable to be arrested in the middle of the night and have their apartment ransacked by the police.* The Dutch people must be scratching their heads wondering what ever happened to the free country they used to live in before Islam came along.

* As happened to cartoonist Gregorius Nekschot in May 2008.

Last week in the football tournament, when the Dutch team lined up for their national anthem, I was half expecting to hear the Muslim call to prayer ringing out around the stadium. Is that offensive? I do hope so, because it's time to stop being polite. It's time to stop showing fake respect and to start insisting that this divisive dangerous insulting poisonous bullshit is taken out of our public life, where it violates our human rights. Out of the government, out of the law, and especially out of education.

And all the vast army of self-interested money-grubbing clergy and lobby groups, and other assorted faith-based so-called community leaders who currently feed on our freedom like maggots should be told exactly what they can do with themselves in the bluntest possible terms. I'll even volunteer for that job myself.

Peace, but not at any price.

43

Islam Is Not a Victim

July 20, 2008

First of all I need to apologise to anyone from the religion of peace who has sent me a death threat recently. I'm afraid I haven't been able to respond, unfortunately, because I get so many messages and e-mails from sane people that it takes up all my time in replying to as many of them as I can, so if you haven't heard from me please don't think I'm being rude, because I would hate to cause offence.

I suppose I should have realised that some people would fly off the handle at being told that they can't take criticism. I can take criticism, which is just as well, because I get called a racist and an Islamophobe almost every single day; not to mention a Jew, a homosexual, and various other names that some Muslims seem to think are insults, when in fact they're not.

And I don't mind. You won't find me running to a tribunal or a human rights commission to whine and whinge about it for financial gain, unlike some delicate souls we could mention.

But one thing that does bother me is the fact that some people seem to think I've got something against all Muslims, which simply isn't true.

Anyone who has seen my videos knows very well that I've got no problem with anyone, no matter what they believe, who doesn't want to interfere with my freedom. (And that includes freedom from religion, of course – that's all religion, all the time.)

And I know there are plenty of Muslims who agree with me about that because some of them actually write to me and tell me so, and I'm very grateful for their support. But just because those people are enlightened it doesn't mean Islam itself is benign, or should be trusted, because unfortunately right now the cutting edge of Islam is in other hands, and those hands are a lot less enlightened and a lot more dangerous.

The royal family of Saudi Arabia, a small coterie of people unelected by anybody, have hijacked that country's vast oil wealth, and are using it to force the very worst of Islam into the free world.

So far they've spent one hundred billion dollars building mosques and funding pressure groups of fanatics who install themselves in western society under grand official sounding titles full of words like congress and council, and then claim to speak for all Muslims, while in reality doing all they can to stop Muslims from integrating, because their existence and their income depend on keeping Muslims separate and in conflict with everybody else.

So, when it's claimed, as it was last week on British television, that Muslims in Britain are victims of British intolerance (yeah, right – sixteen hundred mosques worth of intolerance so far, and still building), I think the truth is, if they are victims of anything, it's Muslim intolerance, because if you are an ordinary Muslim surely the last thing you need is a bunch of Islamists speaking for you. Everything they do and say reflects back on you. When they try to force unwanted Islamic values into our education system, for example, or when one of their representatives crudely insults this country by comparing it with Nazi Germany, that reflects on all Muslims, because these people speak for all Muslims, don't they? No? Well, maybe somebody should tell them that.

To be fair, one thing that really doesn't help is when some patronising multicultural fascist decides to ban something innocuous because they think Muslims would be offended by it. These are the same people, no doubt, who decided that kitchen staff in hospitals and schools have to serve the cruelty of halal meat to everyone, because it's uneconomical to do it separately, and Muslims must never be offended. Or the people who offered Muslim-only days in public swimming pools, excluding everybody else, because it seems that some Muslims actually are offended at having to bathe among kuffars and infidels.

Technically it's not racist of them, because Islam is not a race. So that's OK, then. But anyone who criticises it is a racist, because language means whatever we want it to mean in the topsy-turvy world of multicultural hypocrisy, where everyone in the West is automatically guilty of crimes committed by their ancestors, should be deeply ashamed of their identity, and spend their whole lives apologising for it

There was one particularly silly incident in Dundee recently. You probably saw this story, it was all over the news, where a Muslim councillor took it upon himself to decide that a police poster with a puppy dog on it was offensive to Muslims.

Well, in the event it was wishful thinking on his part because nobody actually gave a damn, but the police went ahead and apologised anyway like a bunch of dhimmis.

Recently the West Midlands police had to fork out substantial damages to the makers of a television film, *Undercover Mosque*, whom they had falsely accused of misrepresenting the intolerant Muslim bigots they exposed.

Now you can't blame the individual police officers for this kind of behaviour, because they're in an impossible situation, under orders from above that political correctness trumps common sense, so they're forced to treat the word Islamophobia as if it's a real word, and as if there's actually something wrong with people who dislike Islam for the sexism, racism and homophobia that run through it like a watermark.

But let's not be too negative here. Occasionally, just occasionally, a small oasis of sanity does emerge from this desert of bollock-brained Islamic appeasement. You may remember those stupid Muslim law students who allowed themselves to be used as sock puppets by the Canadian Islamic Congress in order to exploit that country's insane human rights legislation and stamp out free speech.

Well, the case has been thrown out by the Canadian Human Rights Commission, which is good news, but the British Columbia commission might yet embarrass itself by ruling in their favour. But either way, in bringing this case in the first place, and with the public reaction it's received, these idiots have clearly managed to expose themselves to the hatred and contempt that they had falsely accused *Maclean's* magazine of fostering, and who can say that they haven't earned it with full honours?

They surely deserve all the scorn and derision, and suspicion, that's now bound to follow them around like a vapour trail, because everyone knows their underhand motive in bringing this case had nothing to do with human rights and everything to do with stamping out legitimate criticism of Islam.

They tried to hijack the law to piss on our freedom and the wind blew it back in their faces. You could almost call it a legal suicide bomb, if you wanted to be offensive.

Peace. Now that is a much better idea, don't you think?

44

The Tyranny of Scripture

August 7, 2008

I sometimes think that if Satan existed he couldn't devise a better way of keeping humanity in chains than by encouraging the blind uncritical veneration of scripture, and the fossilisation of human thought.

So, without wishing to be too rude about it, I want to say something now to the handful of people who insist on sending me sometimes quite lengthy passages of scripture. You probably know who you are. Well maybe you don't, and maybe that's part of the problem here, but I don't understand why you do this. You must realise, surely, that I never read a single word of it. I recognise it immediately as scripture, and therefore as worthless. So effectively you are wasting your time. The time it takes you to copy and paste that fantasy fiction and send it to me is time that you could be spending far more profitably doing something that you enjoy, like, oh I dunno, flagellating yourself perhaps, rending your garments, gnashing your teeth, prostrating yourself before a crucifix and crying your eyes out for hours on end. Whatever it is you normally do to relax and unwind.

On the other hand, if it's a genuine neurotic problem that you've got, some kind of obsessive compulsive disorder, well obviously that's different. Then I do sympathise. Please carry on sending as much scripture as you like. But consulting a trained mental health professional might also be quite a good idea, because scripture is not reality. I'm sorry to be the one to break the bad news. It's just scripture, I'm afraid. What's been divinely revealed hasn't been revealed at all. It's been imagined. And if it's all you've got to support your particular version of reality and the god who supposedly created it, then I would suggest that your god is in fact a false god, and every time you proclaim him you merely proclaim yourself deceived, like the village idiot who walks around blowing a whistle at people because he thinks it makes him important, when all it does is single him out as the village idiot.

Apologies, by the way, to any genuine idiots who are offended at being associated with religion. That wasn't my intention.

I also get quite a lot of e-mails from secret atheists – people who live in the American Bible Belt and who tell me that they would literally lose their livelihood if the ignoramuses around them knew that they didn't believe in the tribal god of the ancient Judean desert.

In fact, I wouldn't be surprised if there were as many secret atheists in the Bible Belt as there are secret homosexuals in Saudi Arabia.

Well, it's just that with all the available women in that country safely under lock and key where they belong, all those poor studs can turn to is porn or each other – let's be realistic.

But both of these unfortunate groups, the secret atheists and the secret homosexuals, are victims of other people's rigid interpretation of scripture, because scripture gives us licence, if we are that way inclined, to show the very worst of ourselves and to behave in ways we might otherwise be ashamed of if we had any decency about us. There's nothing you can't read into it, or take from it, so whatever nasty shitty little attitude you harbour towards your fellow man will find justification in scripture. Because, like the sands of the desert, fixed and immutable, yet ever shifting, the words of God are infinitely versatile. Open that book and watch them dance across the page like ninjas, each one a soldier for you and your petty prejudices.

But don't make the mistake of thinking that you can blame scripture for your noxious opinions. You can seek refuge in it as many hypocrites do, but you can't hide behind it.

Because scripture depends on interpretation, because it is so ambiguous, the way that you choose to interpret it reveals who you are in your heart. So in that sense it's not a shield at all. It's a spotlight that shows up an evil heart like an x-ray.

As with those hardline Saudi clerics, for example, who take sadistic pleasure interpreting the Koran as cruelly as possible. They merely reveal themselves for the bloodthirsty monsters they are, and advertise to the world the darkness in their petty little souls and their pitiful inadequacy as men.

Right now the Anglican Church is tearing itself apart because some people again have taken refuge in scripture as an excuse for prejudice against women and homosexuals. In any other walk of life in the civilised world this would be prosecuted as a crime. But scripture legitimises it, implying that it's the result of profound reflection, when in fact it's just a grubby front for chauvinism and ignorance. Which brings me back to the Bible Belt, widely recognised, of course, as an area of outstanding natural stupidity, and with very good reason. Especially when you consider the millions of dollars that have been spent in building creation museums. Just think of the psychotherapy that money could have paid for.

Creation museums are the latest symptom of Christi-insanity to hit the United States, and they are, of course, inspired one hundred percent by scripture. At the moment they seem to be popping up like mushrooms, in a spontaneous eruption of life, ironically enough, all over the land of the free, and beyond now.

These are places of education where Christian children can go to learn the truth, that their parents are morons, and quite possibly insane. They'll learn that Adam and Eve not only existed in all their Disney-like fig-leafed apple-chomping glory, but they rode around the place on dinosaurs. Hell, they probably even had rodeos. Well, why not? They were Christians, weren't they?

The dinosaurs died out eventually, and who could be surprised? Look at the company they had to keep. Although one dinosaur is still with us, unfortunately, and that is creationism's very own Ignoramus Rex, a small brained creature with a hard outer shell impervious to reason. It feeds exclusively on scripture, and its copious droppings have not only been used to build these museums, but can serve as a useful metaphor for everything in them.

If you've got a head full of scripture then what you've got is a head full of ideas that have stopped growing. That'll be a head full of dead ideas, then.

And you have no right to have those ideas respected or taken seriously. You're simply not entitled to it.

And you've certainly got no business using them to tell other people how they should live their lives, because you don't know anything.

If patriotism is the last refuge of the scoundrel, scripture is the first refuge of the ignoramus. You can study it for years without learning anything, but you will end up with a lot to say for yourself, and it will all amount to the same thing: Talk to the scripture, cos the brain ain't listening.

Peace, especially to all the secret atheists and homosexuals. Better days are coming.

45

Take Your God and Shove Him

August 21, 2008

OK, you don't need to be religious to be a public nuisance any more than you need a medical degree to be an alcoholic, but statistically it does help, apparently, and who could be surprised?

This is going to be a fairly rude video, because I thought I had made my position on scripture fairly clear the last time, but apparently not. There are some people who have decided to evangelise to me, because in their opinion I haven't quite grasped the truth, and they want to set me straight about that, using guess what, scripture. And because I don't want to hear any of this, I'm closed-minded, apparently, which is a novelty. Being called closed-minded by religious people is a bit like being called yellow by a bunch of bananas.

But in this case I have to admit there's some truth in the accusation. The fact is I'm so closed-minded that I'm only prepared to engage with reality.

I know it sounds unreasonable, but if something isn't real then

I find I've got an inbuilt automatic prejudice – that's right, a prejudice – against pretending that it is real.

In fact I'm so closed-minded when it comes to believing absurdities that, you won't believe this, but I actually require proof. That's right, copper-bottomed proof that would stand up in a court of law. A real court, not a human rights commission. And we both know that you and your scripture are not going to furnish that proof if you talk from now until the end of time. So let's not bother and say we did, because you'd be far better employed reflecting on the fact that your deeply held beliefs are really nothing more than an accident of birth. The parents that you happened to be born to and the stuff they happened to believe in is now doubtless what you believe in. Had you been born elsewhere you'd believe other stuff, and this stuff you would consider heretical and false.

Yet in both cases yours would be the only true religion. How are you not embarrassed?

So no, thank you, I don't want to hear about your beliefs, and I don't give a damn what your scriptures have to say about anything. Sorry to be so closed-minded, but I'm going to spell it out for you now as clearly as I can, just to avoid any future misunderstandings. I don't care if you've got a written formula for converting lead into gold. Keep it to yourself.

Evangelising to people who don't want to hear it is such a tasteless thing to do. It's like exposing yourself in public. Whatever happened to good manners? It's not as if we don't even know the pitch. God knows we've heard it thousands and thousands of times, and it doesn't get any more convincing in the telling, but that doesn't seem to register with you, does it?

If somebody tried to sell me a car and I decided it wasn't for me, I wouldn't expect that person to return the following day and try to sell it to me again, especially if it was an invisible car. If they did, they would be dismissed in very short order, and they would not be given any respect.

Because, you see, I'm not in the market for a car. Any car. I've decided to walk. That's going to take me where I'm going, because I'm going where it takes me. And I'll be happy to get there. In fact, I already am.

So I don't need to hear about anybody's god or saviour or prophet or scripture or any sort of supernatural deity hocus pocus whatsoever, or even any fancy variation on that theme, half man half god kind of arrangements. I'm not interested. I've heard it all before and I think it's all lies. Insulting degrading nonsense that contaminates everything it touches. In fact, whenever I'm exposed to religion I feel dirty. I feel contaminated by the vileness of the mealy-mouthed platitudes that pass for wisdom, the naked money-grubbing, the controlling rhetoric devoid of any humanity or compassion – are you kidding me? The supercilious hectoring tone, the constant intrusive demands for privilege, and the absolutely unforgivable violation of the minds of young children, and I think those people who make a profession of religion are the scum of the earth. And I think that if Jesus turned up tomorrow he would agree with me, so let's hope he does. Peace.

46

Islam's War on Freedom

August 31, 2008

Free speech is not a bargaining chip. It's not something for lawyers to dissect to their advantage or for politicians to trade away for cheap votes. It's sacred. And that's a concept that some religious people seem to have trouble understanding.

Just when we thought the United Nations couldn't get any more useless, something called the Organisation of Islamic Conference, which is a fancy way of saying a Saudi-funded cartel of Islamic dictatorships, has been allowed to hijack the United Nations Human Rights Council, thus rendering it instantly and permanently worthless.

Nevertheless, with all the plodding predictability of a Hollywood car chase, their first order of business was to pass a resolution banning criticism of Islam and sharia, and, by extension, of their own barbaric regimes, with all the stonings and beheadings, amputations and female genital mutilation that so disgusts everyone in the civilised world.

In other words they've tried to make it illegal to criticise evil. A bit like abolishing penicillin because the bacteria are offended.

I thought the United Nations existed to help drag countries like this out of the Stone Age, not for them to drag everybody else back there. But apparently not, because next April in Geneva the United Nations is hosting a conference on racism at which this manipulative nonsense is likely to be enshrined, giving Islam special status in international law. And given the kind of unprincipled leaders we have in the West right now, especially here in Europe, there's every chance that this could have a real effect on our freedom of expression in the civilised world.

Islam has a notoriously one-sided view of free speech, just it has a one-sided view of everything else. If you criticise Islam publicly you will be abused and threatened almost beyond belief, as an army of hysterical brainwashed illiteramuses line up to shit the contents of their minds into your mailbox. Check out the feedback page on my website for an idea of what you can expect.

And maybe some of you leftie liberal multicultural pricks who are always telling me that Islam is peace, maybe you'd like to take a look as well, that's if you can bear to pull your heads out of your America-hating arses for five minutes.

"Islam is peace" is a message that has been spread to the four corners of the mosque, and that's where it stops, because nobody else is buying it in a million years. Islam is as Islam does, and as long as the Saudis hold the reins and continue to finance extremists and to teach children violence and hate, then Islam is Islam, and peace has nothing to do with it. And every concession we make to it is an invitation to the past to reach out a bony hand and grab us by the nuts.

And we're already on a slippery slope, which is being liberally greased by our own leaders who don't like freedom any more than Islam does. And that's why Islamists are free to say whatever they want to in our society; to criticise us, to insult us for the way we dress, for the way we behave, our culture, our values, even calling for homosexuals to be killed without being arrested for incitement to murder, because that might inflame community relations. But anyone who so much as raises an eyebrow in protest at any of this is immediately accused of hate speech.

Well, personally, I don't do hate speech, because I think hate is a self-destructive emotion, and therefore rather a stupid one, but I do a pretty good line in disdain and contempt speech, and anyone who thinks their faith should trump my freedom is going to get that by the bucketload. Sorry to be so disrespectful and everything. It's just that I believe the time to start defending your freedom is while you've still got it, not after it's gone. And that's why I think that this conference in Geneva should be boycotted by all civilised countries. The Canadians, to their credit, have already opted out. Let's just hope some pin-headed human rights commissioner doesn't force them to change their minds.

We've been exposed to Islam up close in the West for a couple of decades, I suppose, ever since the Rushdie affair brought it to everyone's attention like a shovel to the back of the head. And we've had a chance to take a good long look at it from our perspective, and to measure it against our cultural values. Remember them?

And many of us don't like what we see, I'm afraid. In fact, we're appalled and disgusted by much of what we see, and we're going to say so loud and clear (well some of us are anyway), and anyone who doesn't want to hear it had better shut their ears along with their minds, because free speech is our birthright in the civilised world. It's what made us the civilised world. And we know it's our lifeline to the future, and if we let anyone pick it apart then our society has no future, which is exactly what the Islamists intend.

Make no mistake, what the people behind this resolution want is to turn this planet into a prison camp, into a worldwide religious police state like Saudi Arabia is today. And that's not a fantasy; it's a reality where women are treated as property, minorities abused and victimised, where execution or mutilation await anyone who steps out of line, where there's no other religion allowed, and where there's no beer! – and just on its own that would be enough for me, quite frankly.

And if we carry on as we have been in the West, staying silent about this, either through fear or through misplaced cultural sensitivity, if we keep letting ourselves be bullied and pushed around by radical Islam and its fellow-travelling multiculturalist pimps, then little by little, resolution by phoney bullshit resolution, our freedom will be eaten away until it's no longer recognisable as freedom at all. At which point you may wake up and look around wondering: "What the hell happened there?" as some bearded ignoramus hands you a one-way ticket back to the seventh century. Enjoy.

Peace, and happy days.

47

Welcome to Saudi Britain

September 30, 2008

Hi everyone. You may remember that a couple of weeks ago it was revealed that sharia courts are now operating here in Britain with the full backing of the law, even though they discriminate against women as a matter of course. And what this means is that those women who are intimidated into using these courts (as some of them will be, and everyone knows it), they will now find that they have the full weight of the British legal system lined up against them alongside the patriarchal bigotry in their own communities.

Those women who are cheated out of their just entitlement in these places, as some already have been, will find that they have no recourse to the real law to put things right.

In other words, we are now accommodating Saudi Arabian legal principles here in Britain, just as we accommodate their corrupt business practices and their threats against our national security when we try to investigate them.

If you live in Britain and if you think these courts are a bad idea, please sign the petition to which I've linked, asking that they be abolished and that this poison be removed from our society, and that we revert to the rule of civilised law with equal rights for all, if that's not too much trouble.

Over the last eleven years of this Labour government we've had in Britain, the British people have seen their society subjected to social engineering on a massive scale by a misguided and arrogant liberal elite who, in their eagerness to fragment the fabric of our society, have actually succeeded in giving civilised values a bad name.

Tolerance and diversity are good things on paper. I'm sure we'd all vote for tolerance and diversity. But in practice they've become a nightmare of doublethink and lies, where the most unreasonable people in society are encouraged at every turn to be even more unreasonable.

A case in point, just this week some idiot from Saudi Arabia is being allowed to sue a supermarket because he was required to handle alcohol as part of his job, despite being told this when he took the job. And despite the fact that thousands of Muslims in Britain handle alcohol every day when they sell it in their corner shops to people like me.

I do find it quite ironic that Islam forbids intoxication when you consider how many Muslims are seemingly so intoxicated by their religion, especially in Saudi Arabia. So it was no surprise to me to hear that this idiot was from Saudi Arabia, because I think we all know that entire country is mentally ill.

The Saudis would have us believe that theirs is the purest form of Islam. Well, I don't know about that, but it's certainly the nuttiest form. It's barking mad, if you'll pardon the canine metaphor. And it's pig-ignorant, even if you won't.

It's got to be just about the nastiest belief system on this faith-obsessed planet. And it's a cowardly one as well, enforced by cowardly men who are afraid of women, and whose only language is ultimately violence. They're absolutely pathetic, and history is already laughing at them.

If the term "human rights" means anything in this world, then one day the Saudis will pay out as much in compensation for their abuse of women as the Catholic Church has for its abuse of children. And I'll certainly drink to that.

I was out earlier today, coincidentally, buying some beer. Not because I enjoy beer particularly, but because I know it offends Islam. Although it didn't seem to bother the Muslim shopkeeper I bought it from. Maybe he was just being polite.

Anyway, as I was leaving the shop with my beer, two women happened to walk past wearing burkas. Nothing too unusual about that, not any more, not in London anyway, and nobody really paid it much attention, apart from one small child who I overheard describing them to her mother as letterbox ladies, which I thought was actually quite inventive and rather charming.

But of course it was also deeply offensive, so we had the child put to death.

No, not really. But it was lucky that neither of the women actually heard the offensive and insulting remark, because obviously each of them had her head encased in a cloth sack, so that was good, because it meant that the police didn't have to be called, no human rights people needed to get involved, and nobody required any financial compensation for hurt feelings, which I thought made a very pleasant change indeed.

And, of course, as a result, we didn't have to listen to any propaganda soundbites from some Islamist Saudi shill at the Muslim Council of Britain.

So all in all it worked out for the best. And it just goes to show that these things don't always have to end in tears.

Peace, especially to everyone who remembers to sign the petition.

48

Stop Sharia Law in Britain

October 6, 2008

Well, first of all I want to thank everyone who helped get my last video reinstated on YouTube. I'm very grateful to everyone for their support on that. I want to thank YouTube as well, obviously, for reinstating it, but most of all I want to thank all those people who flagged the video in the first place, for giving us all a bit of fun, and for taking a dump in their own oatmeal, because it's thanks to those people that that video is now all over the internet and all over YouTube like a rash, which just goes to show what can be achieved when we all work together. Thanks guys.

I was told that it was removed because it violated YouTube's guidelines on hate speech, in particular where I referred to the entire country of Saudi Arabia as mentally ill. So let me just clarify that point now to avoid any future confusion.

It's my belief that the laws which govern the country of Saudi Arabia are insane and wicked laws, and that the people who enforce them are seriously mentally ill.

Of course there are people in Saudi Arabia who disagree with those laws and who would rather things were different in that country, and I wouldn't mind betting that the majority of those people are female.

However, they still have to live in a society which is governed with an iron rod by superstitious barbarians and policed by violent fanatics. In other words, a society which is, in fact, mentally ill.

And, as if to illustrate the black hole of sexual repression that is Saudi Arabia, just this week a senior Saudi cleric, an Islamic "scholar", if you'll pardon the expression, has said that women who wear the burka should show only one eye, not two, because showing two eyes could make a woman seductive, and tempt some unfortunate man into raping her through no fault of his own.

And it's this kind of attitude that governs Saudi Arabia, and convinces me that Saudi Arabia's influence on this planet is a thoroughly cancerous one, and the worst advertisement for any religion that it would be possible to imagine.

Even Scientology looks good next to the Wahhabi doctrine, a twisted malignant mutation of Islam, which is as vile and as inhuman an ideology as Nazism.

And that's really all I was trying to say.

I also believe that the sharia courts which have been established here in Britain, and which reflect the mentally ill laws of Saudi Arabia, are the thin end of an ever thickening wedge of Islamic medievalism that's being hammered up our fundament by the Saudis with the connivance of our own government.

Our prime minister wants London to be the sharia banking capital of Europe. I'm not sure why. Maybe he's got a side bet with the Dutch and the Swedish governments to see who can completely Islamicise their societies first. Either way, they say money talks, and right now in Britain it's talking Arabic.

But I guess that's what happens, isn't it, when the most backward society on the planet happens to be one of the wealthiest. They can simply bribe their values into places where they don't belong, and where they wouldn't be tolerated for a second if not for their money.

Saudi money is responsible, not just for forcing the British government to cravenly break its own laws, not just for the various pressure groups of Islamist fanatics who claim to speak for all Muslims in Britain, but also for the hundreds of mosques that have been established here in recent years, including the one in London that was exposed recently on television for allowing hate speech to be preached in its purest form – specifically that Muslims should hate anyone who isn't a Muslim, and that apostates and homosexuals should be killed. They couldn't quite make up their minds whether these people should be thrown from the top of a mountain or stoned to death, or both, leaving another tricky theological poser for the "scholars".

But allowing these courts into Britain is not just pandering to Saudi money, is it? It's also a cynical, and I think quite typical vote-whoring tactic by the Labour Party, of which I'm ashamed to admit I used to be a card-carrying member. Now I wouldn't vote Labour again at gunpoint, because like many people, over the last eleven years I've realised that a vote for Labour is a vote for Islam.

And although I like and admire certain individual Muslims as people, I've seen enough of Islam to know that I don't want it anywhere near me. And I don't want any of its values enshrined in the laws of the country I live in. I want to see Islam relegated to its rightful place in society as a non-influential non-intrusive spiritual belief system. And that's really what this petition was all about. It did quite well in the short time we managed to publicise it, but now it's closed. However, there is a new petition which runs until the end of the year, which should give everyone the chance to spread it around far and wide.*

If people know about this they will sign it, because you know that all your friends are just as sick as you are of having Islam rammed down their throats and being called racists if they complain about it. So maybe this time we can get enough signatures to make this genuinely newsworthy and give this disgraceful government the kick in the crotch it's been asking for.

Oh, and if the people who flagged the last video could do me a huge favour and flag this one as well, I'd be most grateful. Thanks again for all your help. Peace.

---

* A petition can still be signed at onelawforall.org.uk.

49

Godless and Free

October 31, 2008

Somebody pointed out to me recently that by focussing on what I don't want, namely religion, I'm attracting more of it into my life, which I agree would be a very unfortunate irony, if not for the fact that I'm focussing on what I do want, and that's freedom, and lots of it.

You see, I make these videos, not because I despise religion as humanity's way of poking itself in the eye with a sharp stick for no reason, although obviously I do, but because I want to live in a free world full of free people who can say whatever they want to say, and who can be whoever they want to be, one thousand percent of the time, and where nobody is allowed to shut them up because their crackpot religious beliefs have been offended.

I don't care at all about theology, unless it threatens that freedom, and then I care about it the way I care about rabies or typhoid. So you could say that I'm not so much anti-religion as pro-freedom. Indeed, if religion was pro-freedom I wouldn't have such a problem with it, but then if religion was pro-freedom it wouldn't exist, because religion feeds on a broken spirit. That's why it tries to break your spirit the moment you come into contact with it.

Submit, obey, do not question. Those words should be chiselled above the entrance of every church and every mosque, because that's the only message religion has when it comes right down to it: Praise the Lord, or else.

The Pope spelled it out for American Catholics when he told them: "Obedience to the doctrine of the Church is the foundation of your faith." That's what he said. There was no mention of enlightenment or spirituality or any of these things, because he's not in that business. He's in the obedience business, the only business where the customer is always wrong.

Clergy are the only salesmen who don't have to justify or prove any of the outrageous claims they make for the product they're hustling, and this leaves them free to engage in the kind of open fraud which in any other walk of life would be a criminal offence.

For the level of investment they demand from us, I believe we're entitled to expect actual enlightenment and wisdom in return. Instead what do we get? We get dogma, crude coercion and endless empty pieties about the love of a god who clearly loves us the way a violent husband loves the woman sitting next to him with two black eyes. If we step out of line we pay in the most brutal way.

And it's this crass violence at the heart of religion which I believe makes it truly evil, and also furnishes proof, as if proof were needed, that this is an entirely manmade phenomenon with nothing divine about it, otherwise it wouldn't be so damned ugly.

The god of the desert is transparently a false god. He's a puppet who speaks with the voice of ignorant men who are afraid of knowledge and afraid of freedom, and who therefore need desperately to control the thoughts of others for their own miserable survival.

They need us to believe that we're less than we are, and to diminish ourselves in our own minds; to feel small, helpless, in need of salvation. So what do they tell us? They tell us that strength and virtue lie in submission. Yes, of course they do. With our faces in the dust we are invincible, isn't that right? And of course we will live forever, either in eternal bliss or in eternal torment, but that's entirely up to us.

Eternal bliss requires that you wear a straitjacket of blind faith, not permanently, just from now until you die. Whereas living a joyful humane compassionate but godless life will get you horribly tortured for all eternity.

Fear is religion's currency of choice. It's the lowest of human emotions, because it's the most crippling emotion, and that's why it's religion's currency of choice. It's pretty obvious when you think about it, but hey, don't strain yourselves.

But actually it's religion that has everything to fear, because it depends on maintaining the illusion, maintaining the spell, and hoping that nobody manages to burst its artificial bubble of faith. And this is exactly why it wages such determined war on our basic freedoms of thought and speech. But it's losing this war, because every day more and more of us are waking up to the damage that this nonsense is doing to our world. We can see our societies being twisted out of shape, being injected with false values that pander to bigotry and superstition, and we've realised that this god of the desert has outstayed his welcome and become a liability, and quite frankly he needs us a lot more than we need him, because we've moved on from the desert, and we've discovered a few things about the world and the universe and our place in it, and we're no longer afraid of the thunder and lightning. Our world is no longer populated by demons and hobgoblins, and we no longer need to be led around by the nose for the benefit of clergy.

And they know this, just as they know that their god's very existence depends entirely on our belief – belief without evidence and belief that defies reason.

And when that belief disappears, as one day it certainly will, this ridiculous god will disappear with it, instantly and forever.

He won't be able to vent his wrath or visit retribution on anyone, because he won't exist. He'll evaporate quicker than common sense in a creation museum, and his vast army of controlling parasitical clergy will find themselves briefly cartoon-like in mid air, before dropping like fleas into a bucket.

That's what I'm looking forward to, and that's what I'm focussed on, and it's why I make these videos, because I think we're better than this, and I know we've got the power to withdraw our belief and our consent and put a stop to this nonsense – all we need is the courage.

Peace, and freedom. Let's not forget the freedom.

50

The Water of Life

December 23, 2008

Hi everyone. As some of you may know I've been away for a while on a drugs binge.* Not only that, it was an atheist drugs binge, which makes it a thousand times worse. At least I hope it does. But now that I'm back in some kind of reasonable shape, I just thought I'd make this video, firstly to wish everybody a merry Christmas whether they like it or not, and also to answer a couple of points that people have made to me recently.

Somebody said: "You know, you're not going to win the battle of ideas by insulting people you disagree with." Which is a fair point. Or it would be if we were engaged in a battle of ideas, but unfortunately religion doesn't have ideas. It has dogma. And the purpose of dogma is to get in the way of ideas; to stamp them out and kill them off before they succeed in changing anything. Because, as everyone knows, change to religion is pretty much

* This is a reference to pain killers I had been prescribed for a temporary back problem. I mentioned it because several people had kindly asked how I was doing.

what kryptonite is to Superman. It's about as welcome as garlic to a vampire, because it threatens the position of those who control religion for their own narrow ignorant selfish ends.

And secondly, I don't insult people because I disagree with them: people who believe in, say, things like spiritualism or astrology, even though I don't believe in those things myself (although I have to say I think the planets do influence our lives, mainly by not crashing into us, which I think is quite considerate of them, really). But if astrologers were demanding special privileges all the time, and insisting that their beliefs be allowed to dictate the behaviour of others, then I'd probably adopt rather a different tone.

If astrologers enjoyed a tax exempt status which they routinely abused to meddle in politics and force their values into other people's lives, or if they reacted with fury, threatening to kill people at the slightest criticism of their beliefs, or if astrologers were allowed to indoctrinate young children before their minds were fully formed, and if they then molested many of these children and protected each other from justice, while insisting that women and homosexuals not be allowed to practice astrology because they're women and homosexuals, well then one or two insults might slip out. That's how it works.

And I don't apologise for that. Why should I, when religion has the barefaced cheek to claim moral authority over us when anyone can see it doesn't even have any moral awareness? How can it have, when it's so insulated from self-examination by its blind obedience to scripture?

It seems like hardly a week goes by these days that we don't have to listen to some mealy-mouthed clergyman complaining that secularism is going to lead to moral anarchy and the breakdown of society, as if people really are stupid enough to swallow this shallow-minded self-serving bullshit.

Obviously nobody wants to live in a moral vacuum. Well, nobody outside politics and banking. But far from filling this vacuum, as it always claims, religion has actually caused it by using scripture as a vacuous substitute for genuine morality, by denying people the chance to formulate their own more substantial moral bearings in the only place that you find anything of real value, and that's within.

If it hasn't come from within it isn't worth a damn, and you know that in your heart. You know it's been put on like a cheap Sunday suit, and it's as phoney as a clip-on bowtie.

If you get your morals uncritically from scripture you're really no better than a dog who's afraid to steal the meat because he knows he'll be whipped. He'd love that meat more than anything, but, like you, his finely tuned moral compass keeps him on the straight and narrow. What a good dog he is.

Of course a dog doesn't have a soul (apparently) so he doesn't have the problem of having to live forever, but you do, and you know you'll be whipped forever if you even think about touching that meat, you bad dog, you miserable sinner.

Now maybe this doesn't apply to you, because you are, in fact, a happy worshipper. Maybe you embrace the Lord every day with a joyful heart, and that's great, but surely you realise that the moment you change your mind about the Lord and stop embracing him you're setting yourself up for some terrible eternal torture. Don't you ever feel as if somebody is shooting at your feet to make you dance? Because that's how it looks to a neutral observer.

Now maybe that's just my ignorance talking, because that's something else I get accused of quite a lot. Somebody said recently: "Clearly you just don't understand what a person's faith actually means to them. For me," she said, "it's like the water of life."

And I thought: "What a great phrase. The water of life, without which, of course, there can be no life."

But even the water of life needs to be contained and properly managed, or it can run out of control, get into places where it doesn't belong and cause real damage.

For example, if the water of your life gets together with the water of other people's lives and they form a deluge, a rushing torrent of righteous certainty that sweeps all before it, including reason, then it's not so much the water of life any more, is it? It's rapidly turning the water of death, as everything in its path is crushed – original thought, rational enquiry, free speech – and their tattered remnants are strewn upon the rocks of scripture and blind dogma.

What's needed here, obviously, is a dam to contain this water of death, convert it back into the water of life, and give us all a chance to switch on a lightbulb in our minds. And that's where secularism comes in. It's everybody's friend, believer and non-believer alike, which I think makes it the real water of life, at least almost as much as this stuff, beer. Cheers. *(Takes a sip from a glass of exceptionally tasty dark ale.)*

Now that's what I call the water of life.

A merry Christmas to everyone, especially to all you Islamist crackpots who think that celebrating Christmas is a sin. Of course it is. That's why it's fun. Peace.

51

Shame on the Netherlands

January 25, 2009

Well, I suppose it had to happen eventually. The Dutch government is clearly just so determined to prostrate its country towards Mecca that insulting Islam is now officially a criminal offence. That's right. You're not allowed to insult anyone's beliefs in the Netherlands, even if those beliefs insult you and everything you stand for.

As part of the ongoing Islamisation process, the Amsterdam appeals court has sanctioned the prosecution of an elected politician* for making a film critical of Islam and for comparing the Koran with *Mein Kampf*.

Now I have to say I've never actually read Hitler's book, but I have read the Koran, and as an unbeliever (which I am, by the way – I don't know if I've ever mentioned that before) if I talked about Muslims the way their holy book talks about me, I'd be

* Geert Wilders

arrested for hate speech and I'd probably end up in prison.

Fortunately I don't feel inclined to behave in that way because I don't feel the same level of hatred towards Muslims that their holy book evidently feels towards me.

In justifying this prosecution, the court said that it went according to the standards of the European Court of Human Rights, which, I have to say, rang one or two alarm bells, because I think we all know by now that whenever we hear the words "human rights" in connection with Islam we're about to be confronted with another piece of ugly opportunism that spits in the face of genuine human rights and insults everyone's intelligence.

And so it was a few months ago when the Islamic dictatorships hijacked the United Nations Human Rights Council and immediately demanded that western governments make it a crime to criticise Islam.

At the time I didn't know whether the Dutch or the Swedish government would be the first to snap to attention and offer them everything they want on a silver plate, but in the event the Dutch establishment just happened to have a convenient fall guy who they didn't want embarrassing them any more, because let's be fair, they're more than capable of embarrassing themselves.

And what a wonderful job they're doing of that at the moment; embarrassing not only themselves, but their people, their country. In fact the entire continent of Europe is blushing for Holland today, especially for the dhimmi judges of Amsterdam to whom the politics of appeasement are clearly more important even than justice. Shame on you.

And what kind of justice system is it where the truth is inadmissable as evidence? What kind of a place are the Dutch people allowing their country to turn into? From a beacon of enlightened liberal values to the leading edge of the new totalitarianism in just a few short years, thanks entirely to the influence of Islam.

You're being chewed up and spat out, is what's happening to you people. Look at what you're doing. You're prosecuting a man who lives under twenty-four hour protection from attack by violent Muslims, yet he's the criminal for expressing an opinion? Lewis Carroll couldn't have written this one any better.

Nobody should be compelled to respect an ideology that doesn't respect them, and Islam respects nobody. It claims dominion. Respect doesn't come into it. You submit. That's the deal.

The Dutch people are finally waking up to this fact. Sixty percent of them now consider Islam to be a threat to their national identity. Unfortunately none of those people are in power.

The ones who are in power have pretty much backed themselves into a corner – either continue with this toxic multicultural lie indefinitely or admit to a catastrophic mistake in opening the floodgates to Islam in the first place. But they could never do that, because that would be racist. That's quite a predicament, isn't it?

It would funny if it wasn't so tragic. In fact, it's still quite funny, because stupidity in action is always pretty funny. But this is a dark hour for the Netherlands, there's no doubt about that. And it's also kind of a watershed moment for the rest of Europe. We'll all be watching now to see how this turns out. If these charges succeed we'll know the dyke has been breached and it's the beginning of the end of justice as we know it in Europe, and the beginning of creeping sharia, or injustice, as we know it. Looking forward to that? No, me neither.

The truth is sometimes offensive, there's no doubt about that, but it doesn't make it any less true. And the truth is that there are millions of people all over the western world who are absolutely sick and tired of Islam. They're sick of hearing about it, and they're sick of having to make allowances for it that aren't deserved. And they feel enough is enough. And their voices will be heard.

The multicultural mafia can pretend it ain't so, and they can pass all the laws they want to and continue to harass people and shut down internet connections and generally behave like the Gestapo, but it isn't going to work. You can't change people's hearts by force. We are not going to respect Islam until Islam starts to respect us.

But then if that ever happened it wouldn't be Islam any more, and that, in a nutshell, is the problem.

Peace, and good luck Netherlands. You're going to need it.

52

Freedom Go to Hell

February 13, 2009

Well, what a publicity coup for Mr Wilders. The whole thing has been a magnificent success, hasn't it? Millions of people who didn't even know that this film existed have now made a point of seeking it out on the internet, thanks to the stupidity, the incompetence, and the cowardice of the British government.

Of course some of the credit should also go to the idiotic Lord Ahmed who started the whole thing in the first place because he wanted to be a big hero in Pakistan. Unfortunately, the only thing he has managed to achieve is to stereotype Muslims yet again as hysterical intolerant malcontents who can't take criticism, when everybody knows that's not true.

For those who don't yet know, the British government yesterday debased itself and its people in an act of quite breathtaking dhimmitude. An elected parliamentarian from the Netherlands, Mr Wilders, was due to attend the House of Lords for a discussion about his film *Fitna*, but he was turned back at

Heathrow airport because one Muslim member of the House, somebody who, unlike Mr Wilders, hasn't been elected by anybody, was so incensed at the prospect of free and open discussion between free people in a free country that he threatened to mobilise ten thousand angry Muslims to besiege Parliament illegally if Mr Wilders was allowed to attend.

So what do you think the British government did in the face of this open threat to public order? Oh go on, have a guess. That's right, they caved in like a bunch of spineless pussies. I couldn't have put it better myself.

The last thing they needed was an angry Muslim demonstration on their hands, because then the police would have had to go around arresting people who complained about the violent hate-mongering slogans and the offensive anti-Semitic chanting, and that might have been a little embarrassing.

I think it's pretty clear to most of us by now that religious censorship is moving towards us in the free world like an incoming tide, and if we don't do something about it soon we're going to find ourselves cut off like a bunch of stranded cockle pickers.

Since my last video, a number of people contacted me to point out that one reason why the Netherlands is surrendering so completely to Islam is because the government there is controlled by Christians to whom religion is more important than community harmony, and to whom any religious values in society are better than none.

In other words, if you vote for Christians in Holland at the next election, don't bother crossing yourself, because you're actually voting for Islam, and you can wave your open tolerant society a permanent goodbye.

In Britain we've known for some time that a vote for Labour is very much a vote for Islam. The Labour Party depends on the Muslim vote to have any chance at all of staying in power at the next election, because they've alienated just about everybody else.

And the ugly surveillance society they've foisted on us over the last twelve years tells us that the Labour Party despises freedom almost as much as Islam does, which is why they make such willing bedfellows, although not in a gay way. I don't want to insult anyone's homophobic prejudices, because that might cause offence.

But, as if to illustrate this fact, a government minister actually praised Muslims in Britain recently for raising the profile of religion because, as he put it, secular commentators are afraid to criticise them. That's right. It's a good thing that people have been intimidated into silence in New Labour's new Islamic Britain; that the threat of Muslim violence, which is what we're actually talking about here, let's be completely frank about this, has been a good thing for this country. Well, "freedom go to hell" indeed.

You know, maybe I'm naive, but I'm actually astonished that in twenty-first-century Europe we find ourselves having to defend our freedom in our own countries, not only from religious fascists who want to take it away, but from those among us who want to help them do it.

I don't think the Koran should be banned, but also I don't think it should be protected from criticism the way it has been here, in this cowardly way.

This issue cuts to the very foundations of our society. Free speech is the cornerstone of western civilisation. It has made us what we are, and without it we are nothing, and that's precisely why it's under such sustained attack from the footsoldiers of Islam.

If these people are afraid of this film, and clearly they are, it means they're afraid of their own scripture. They know it can't be defended. They know that what the film says is actually true, unpalatable though it may be. Watch it for yourself, it's only a few minutes long, and see if you disagree with a single frame. And then ask yourself how much more of your freedom needs to be whittled away to defend this intolerant misogynistic homophobic anti-Semitic ideology from the robust and frank and open criticism that it so richly deserves.

Peace. Well, we can all dream, can't we? Or is that illegal too now?

53

A Word About the Soldiers

March 12, 2009

OK, I just want to say something quickly here about that little gang of bearded pinheads who abused the British soldiers while they were parading through Luton the other day on their return from Iraq.*

These people couldn't have made their religion look any uglier, any more sordid, if they tried.

Like a lot of people in Britain, I'm against the war in Iraq, have been all along, but I realise that soldiers don't start wars, soldiers don't decide what wars to fight, and frankly, the soldiers of this country already get enough abuse from their own government without this shit on top. Sent into battle under-equipped because some fat-arsed bureaucrat can't stop picking his nose long enough to do his job properly, it's a wonder

---

* British soldiers returning from Iraq were publicly abused by a small group of loudmouthed Islamist boneheads, and the handful of bystanders who tried to challenge them were arrested. I was pretty annoyed about it, as you can see.

anybody joins the army any more. But you know something? I'm glad that they do.

You see, I'm lucky enough never to have had to fight in a war, because other people fought my wars for me – important wars that needed to be won – and I'm very grateful for that. And if you live in this country, and if you accept everything that this country has to offer, which is a lot, then they fought your wars too, whether you bloody well like it or not.

And if you're offended by the sight of British soldiers parading in uniform through a British town, then I would suggest that you don't belong in this country, and I don't care what colour you are, what you believe, or where you were born. Goodbye.

54

Free Speech Is Sacred

March 17, 2009

It's at times like this, isn't it, that you realise just how much we need the United Nations – about as much as we need an ear infection.

You probably know by now that a cartel of Islamic dictatorships has taken time out from abusing human rights to hijack the UN Human Rights Council, which is now dominated by the kind of countries that everybody wants to get out of but nobody wants to get into. And they intend to use an upcoming conference in Geneva to force through a resolution that will criminalise the defamation of religion.

That's quite a specific charge, isn't it, "the defamation of religion", though I'm sure it was intended to be anything but.

To defame something, first of all you have to say something untrue about it, so, for example, if I say that religion is the art of sugar-coating a turd and selling it as a doughnut, that's not defamation because, of course, it is absolutely true

Also, defamation means to damage someone's reputation with falsehood, but since religion's reputation couldn't really be any lower than it is right now – I mean it really stinks, doesn't it? I mean REALLY stinks.

For example, if you're a Catholic you found out last week that you can be excommunicated for helping a child have an abortion,* but not for impregnating her in the first place. Doesn't that stink? Isn't that like somebody just ran over a skunk outside your house?

The only actual defamation I can detect here is defamation of humanity by religion, because religion is bearing false witness against us to our detriment. And that is defamation.

Religion is telling us a poison story about ourselves because it doesn't want us to like ourselves one little bit. So it denigrates us from the moment we're born as unworthy, unclean, and stained with sin; persuading us that there's something we need to be saved from, and indeed there is – the curse of religion, which, for its very survival, depends on keeping us in thrall to a view of reality that's so childish, so stunted, so utterly and transparently false it amounts to nothing less than a malicious assault on our very identity as human beings, which I believe makes religion a crime against humanity.

Now I'd like to be charitable and to attribute this cynical stunt to a lack of understanding by the Islamic dictatorships – a lack of sensitivity if you like, an ignorance if you prefer, a gross ignorance if you insist – about just how unforgivably

* As happened to the mother and doctors of a nine-year-old girl in Brazil who had a life-saving abortion. The man who raped her was not excommunicated.

offensive this resolution is to freedom worshippers like myself.

You see, if religious values are to trump everything in this world as they currently seem to be doing, then I claim free speech as my religion. Yes, I'll have a slice of that pie too, thank you, along with all the attendant rights and privileges, of course. Because I can assure you that I venerate free speech as highly as anybody on this planet venerates their god or their scripture or their prophet, and any attempt to suppress free speech is deeply insulting and grossly offensive to me on a personal level. I feel violated to the very core of my being, which seriously hurts my feelings.

Whenever I hear free speech being compromised or restricted, or even heavily criticised, I take that as a grave personal affront and as a grotesquely insensitive attack on my most cherished values. Freedom of thought, freedom of speech, freedom of identity – this is my holy trinity. Each one an intrinsic aspect of my god – freedom, the holiest of holies. Yes, it bloody well is. It is absolutely sacred and inviolable beyond any negotiation or compromise, now and forever, amen.

(Sorry to be so unreasonable about it, but you know how it is with religion.)

And in keeping with my sincerely held religious convictions, I even support free speech for those clowns who abused the soldiers in Luton last week. Some people seem to think I wanted them silenced. Not at all. I think everyone should be free to express who they really are and be judged on that. So I fully support their right to make public dicks of themselves if that's what they want to do, and to unite the whole country, Muslim and non-Muslim alike, against them in condemnation.

I also support their right to go and live somewhere more in tune with their noxious, barbaric, disgusting views.

They want this country to be like Saudi Arabia, a theocratic hellhole where women and homosexuals are routinely abused, and where new ideas are considered blasphemy. The kind of society, in fact, that recently sentenced an elderly woman to forty lashes for having her bread delivered by an unrelated male. Doesn't that stink?

And that's how these people want to live. So it follows that they're never going to be happy in a civilised country like Britain. Despite the generous state benefits that they can scrounge here, and they do, they're always going to be miserable here, always going to be in a bad mood, walking around with their long old beardy faces, offended by everything, insulted by everything, jumping up and down at the roadside at every opportunity with their stupid little banners, shouting at people. What kind of a life is that?

You'd have to be almost insane, wouldn't you, to want to live in a society that you despise so much when your preferred alternative, a brutal medieval theocracy, is right there for you for the price of a plane ticket.

But as long as they choose to stay here I support their right to speak their minds, such as they are. I also support the right of civilised people to tell them exactly what we think of them as bluntly and directly as we choose to. It's called free speech, and it's sacred.

And it's what the UN Human Rights Council wants to take away from us. It wants to stop us from criticising people like this. It wants to stop us from telling the truth.

And that's why every western government needs to boycott this wretched conference in Geneva, and to treat this despicable resolution and its authors with the undisguised contempt that they deserve.

Also, the Human Rights Council itself might want to think about some urgent sensitivity training for some of its less enlightened members, so that this kind of crass insult to civilised values is never ever repeated.

Peace, and happy resolutions.

55

Islamist Dickhead

March 24, 2009

Some people have a way of getting right up your nose, don't they? One such person is Mr Anjem Choudary, a British born Islamist with a very big mouth and some very harsh opinions about how people should be allowed to live their lives.

And he's been popping up quite a lot in the media recently with his pompous little voice and his bushy little face, so stern, so righteous, telling us all what a corrupt society this is, while fully enjoying all its benefits.

His latest pronouncement is that gay people should be stoned to death. Yes, he's a real charmer

I don't know if he's going to be prosecuted for hate speech for saying this (you know, the way a non-Muslim would be) or if the police think that upholding the law might cause offence and harm community cohesion. You'll have to ask them that, if you can find them.

Meanwhile, he wants beer drinkers like me publicly flogged.

Ouch! Now it gets personal. He wants women forced to dress like nuns, and he wants to see the flag of Allah flying over Downing Street.

With such aggressive opinions a man's bound to have some inner tension. Maybe he needs to relax with a few pints of cider and a couple of spliffs. You know, like in the old days. Because we found out recently that before he became an Islamist dickhead this man was quite the party animal. Alcohol, cannabis, casual sex, pornography – you name it, and he sucked it in and blew it out in bubbles, by all accounts.

They say, don't they, there's nothing quite as bad as the enthusiastic convert, although I have to say it's a shame he's not quite devout enough in his new beliefs to have himself retrospectively stoned to death for that behaviour and do us all a huge favour.

It's fair to say that this man is not well liked in Britain. Although he was born here, if the government were to put him on a plane anyway and dump him in the middle of the desert where he rightly belongs, I bet somebody orbiting in a spacecraft would be able to hear the spontaneous applause emanating from this tiny island.

Because, born here on not, he's about as welcome in this country as a fly is in a kitchen, and he serves the same purpose – a poison-spreading nuisance who makes people sick.

I know a lot of Muslims are embarrassed by this guy. They cringe when they see his name in the media because they know that their faith is about to be portrayed yet again as a religion of fruitcakes and sadists.

But they don't have to worry about that, because everybody knows he's an extremist nutcase. Every time he opens his mouth he proves that calling him pig ignorant is actually an insult to pigs.

He's a walking parody, a laughing stock, a ludicrous cartoon character who speaks for nobody but himself and his own pathetic little coterie of insane medieval pinheads.

And ironically this is what makes him a unifying influence (which of course is the last thing he wants to be) because whatever we believe or don't believe, we can all laugh at this idiot together in a wonderful example of actual community cohesion. You see, there's a first time for everything.

As for the flag of Allah flying over Downing Street, my hunch is that the British flag will still be flying there long after Mr Choudary and his fuzzy-faced friends have come to their senses, had a shave, and are back on the cider and spliffs.

Peace.

56

Children of a Stupid God

May 26, 2009

Hello everyone. I've been away for a while, but I'm glad to be back. Among other things recently I've been spending quite a lot of time out in the open air growing vegetables, enjoying the spring weather, and not believing in God, but not necessarily in that order.

Some people will look at the variety and abundance of nature and see proof of God's existence. Well, I've had a good look recently, and I've seen plenty of proof of nature's variety and abundance, but I haven't seen God anywhere. And that doesn't really surprise me, because I don't think that the violent maniac of the Old Testament would be capable of creating a single radish, let alone an entire world.

For one thing, a god who's afraid of new ideas is certainly no creator. But also his eagerness to be worshipped tells us that he's an extremely shallow individual (which is a little worrying, as we're supposed to be created in his image) and his quickness to violence shows that he's also profoundly stupid. Again, uncomfortably close to home.

Indeed, this god is so limited in scope and so aggressively unsubtle both in word and deed that you could be forgiven for mistaking him for some kind of primitive desert-dwelling tribal human being, and concluding, as I have, that we are not his children at all, but in fact he's our child, and he's a very very bad boy.

Even if I'm wrong about this (and I might be – I'm certainly not infallible, unlike certain other people we could mention) and if God really did create the world, then all I can say is well done God, round of applause for God.

But if he expects to be worshipped on the back of it, then I'm afraid he can go straight to hell, which is where I suspect he originated, if such a place exists, because the god of the Old Testament reads as if he's auditioning for the role of Satan. It would be hard to imagine a more malevolent entity without the aid of a pair of comedy horns and a pitchfork.

Just look at his track record. He comes out of the desert a few thousand years ago killing and smiting with righteous abandon, spawns three religions that absolutely loathe each other, supplies us with scriptures that set us at each other's throats like dogs over trifles, dividing us into us and them, into believers and infidels, ensuring that every one of us will be born with millions of instant enemies.

Thanks to this monster we live in a world divided against itself, where every one of us is an infidel to somebody – including you, no matter what you believe, even if it's nothing, you can be guaranteed that somebody somewhere hates your guts because of it. Welcome to planet earth, the centre of the universe. Enjoy your stay. (Although, apparently, not enjoying it will get you into heaven that little bit quicker.)

Now given this humiliating and, let's be frank, embarrassing situation that we find ourselves in, where, thanks to this ludicrous god, the whole world seems to be in an ever decreasing orbit around the black hole of the Middle East, from which not even light can escape (oh, you've noticed that as well?) maybe civilisation, therefore, is a little too much for us to hope for at this early stage in our development. But wouldn't it be nice if we could at least find some way to resolve the artificial differences that this god has imposed on us without resorting to violence?

I'm sorry, I didn't mean that. I take it back. I don't know what came over me. I was just being silly. I do apologise. Of course violence is the only answer. After all, it's the language of God – that'll be our god, the stupid one, the god of death. "Believe in me or burn in hell. Worship me or I'll send a plague. Little pigs little pigs let me come in or I'll burn your cities to the ground."

And, if it's God's language, and if we're created in his image (which presumably means he's also a gullible superstitious fool, but that's another subject), well then it's bound to be our language as well.

And in truth it's just about the only language we know how to speak to each other when push comes to shove, because everybody knows that the threat of violence is behind all diplomacy, no matter how warm the handshake or how charming the smile. In fact, without it we'd barely be able to relate to each other for the perfectly understandable reason that we're too primitive and stupid. (Obviously, I don't claim to speak for everyone, just the people on this particular planet.)

How stupid are we? Well, look at us, we're a naturally curious race of beings. If we weren't we wouldn't be here. The quest for knowledge is what has driven us forward from day one. Yet we subscribe in our millions to these anaerobic belief systems that purposely limit knowledge, discourage curiosity and sanctify ignorance. Why do we do this to ourselves? What are we afraid of? Is it being alone in a cold and empty universe, is that it?

So we'd rather be subject to a cruel and stupid fascist god than to no god at all, and to cringe under the phoney threat of eternal damnation like a bunch of cowardly muppets.

We'd rather drag ourselves through history, inch by tortuous bloody inch, because we've got this dead weight attached to us, this useless lump of fossilised thought we call religion, this psychological ball and chain that we just can't bring ourselves to cut loose, because this god of ours, he may be stupid, he may be as dumb as a sack of walnut shells, but he can only reflect the intelligence that created him, the poor sod.

It's two thousand years now since Jesus lived, if he lived. Let's assume he did just to annoy a few atheists, but don't tell anybody I said that or I'll be in all kinds of trouble.

And Jesus may have been a good guy in many ways, but he was no saint.

He had his dark side. It's wasn't all loaves and fishes and lilies of the field, was it? He's the one who came up with the idea of eternal damnation in the first place, not God, surprisingly.

No, there's nothing in the Old Testament about anybody simmering in the lake of fire – that was Jesus' idea. Maybe God was just so busy killing and maiming people there and then that it completely slipped his mind, and you could certainly understand that, because he was very busy after all. But you have to wonder why Jesus would take up the slack when he seemed to be doing so nicely with his miracles and his parables and his message of sweetness and light. Why would he feel the need to introduce coercion and threats?

Well, because clearly Jesus was no fool, and he quickly realised that he was talking to stupid ignorant barbarians who, despite his enlightening life-giving message, still needed to be threatened with crude violence to make them behave in a civilised way, and two thousand years later nothing has changed.

Who wouldn't be embarrassed? I'm more than embarrassed, if you want the truth. I'm ashamed. I feel like apologising to the universe for wasting its time. (Must be the Catholic in me coming out now.)

We think we're so advanced, don't we, especially now that science is cutting a dash through eleven dimensions, doing religion's job for it in fact, attempting to illuminate the mystery of life rather than suppress it, but down here on the ground it might as well not be happening. Things are just the same as ever; people still worshipping dumb idols, still fearing evil spirits, still cowering under the angry heavens like a bunch of frightened cavemen.

The only mystery to me is how we can look at ourselves in the mirror without laughing.

Peace, and happy days.

57

Ban the Burka

June 28, 2009

Well, this week there's been quite a lot talk about the burka, or the niqab, or whatever you want to call it. I'm talking about the neurotic need that some women have to walk around everywhere in disguise.

Ever since the French president said it was unwelcome in France, there's been a debate going on here in Britain about whether this ugly mobile tarpaulin should be banned. Although, I have to say that if we were a more honest society, and therefore a more healthy society, there would be no need to ban this ridiculous outfit, because it would already have been ridiculed out of existence.

Most Muslims know full well that the burka has nothing at all to do with their religion. There's nothing in the Koran about women dressing up like Darth Vadar. This is a manifestation of a primitive culture and a primitive mindset that deserves about as much respect and consideration as the beliefs of headhunters.

And as for modesty, please, don't make me laugh. Modest people don't draw attention to themselves by dressing up in a mobile tent just to rub it in the face of a culture they despise, but for some reason insist on living in.

The burka will never be welcome here in Europe, or in the western world generally. It will always cause trouble, and that, I suspect, is why it's being worn.

And there are plenty of good reasons to ban this horrible garment, but for me the best reason is the fact that it would offend Islamists, which I think is always a good idea. If a small group of hysterical bearded fanatics are squealing about Islamophobia, well then you know that somebody is doing something right.

Personally, I would ban it on public transport and in public buildings, and anywhere else that other people are expected to show their face as a matter of course. I also think that shops and banks should be allowed to refuse entry to anybody in disguise. And I think that those women who think it's a good idea to walk around in one of these ridiculous outfits should seriously consider seeing a doctor, not only for themselves, but for their babies, some of whom have been born with rickets because their mothers suffer from chronic vitamin D deficiency through lack of sunlight.

Now personally I've been criticised quite heavily in the past for my attitude to this dehumanising shroud, this cloak of death, this mantle of misery. People have said to me: "You say women should be free to live how they want to and to dress how they like, and yet you have ridiculed those women who choose to cover their face of their own free will. And this makes you a hypocrite, and a racist, and an Islamophobe, and a Jew, and a homosexual, and a filthy kuffar who'll burn in hell, inshallah." Or words to that effect.

Well, quite apart from the obvious security threat posed by the burka, which we don't like to talk about too much out of respect for their religion, even though their religion is our biggest security threat (sorry to all you peaceful Muslims, but we all know that is the unfortunate truth, at least right now)...

But quite apart from that whole issue, the burka is more than just an item of clothing, isn't it? It's a political statement of very determined separation (so much for community cohesion) and it's also a powerful symbol of the status of women in the Muslim world, some of whom, even in this country, have no choice as to whether they are encased in these sartorial prisons.

And that's why I believe that those women who deliberately try to legitimise this sinister garment in the free world to make some kind of cockeyed statement are actively condoning and encouraging the oppression of other women on this planet, for which I think they ought to be thoroughly ashamed of themselves. I think what they're doing is deeply immoral, I think they're traitors to their gender, and as a symbol of their religious or cultural identity they might as well be wearing a yellow star.

I also find it baffling as to why it is that the western feminist voice, usually so assertive and confident, is so muted when it comes to women in Islam. That couldn't have anything to do with cultural relativism looking attractively ethnic once you were all safely home and dry, could it girls? Or maybe it just wasn't a very worthwhile cause after all. I don't know, what do you think? I would like to hear, because the silence so far from feminists has been deafening and shameful. Everybody thinks so. Everybody's wondering where the hell are all the feminists. People even write to me and ask me: "Where are the feminists?" As if I'm supposed to know. I'm just as puzzled as everybody else.

But let me tell you what those shy retiring feminists could and should be saying if they were anywhere to be found, and that is that any western woman who makes allowances for, or who accommodates, the misogyny of Islam in her life is a fool to herself and a traitor to her daughters who will have to live with the consequences in a society where they feel less valued, less safe, and have fewer rights than they do now.

And personally I don't want to be a party to anything like that, and that's why I think that the issue of women's rights should be a line in the sand that Islam is not allowed to cross at any price. The emancipation of women in Islam is one of the most important political issues on this planet because it's the only thing that's likely to civilise this crackpot religion of peace. And I think that western governments who claim to stand for freedom and justice should be pursuing it vigorously and without compromise, regardless of anybody's feelings or cultural sensitivities, especially within their own borders. And that means no sharia, and no burka.

But let's not be too intolerant. That's the worst thing you can be as a modern European, and I'm nothing if not a modern European. So I wouldn't want to ban the burka for absolutely everyone. Not at all. In fact I think it should be compulsory for all Islamist men, especially during the hot weather, and maybe then we'd find out just how popular this thing really is.

Peace, especially to all the silent feminists. You know who you are, even if nobody else does.

58

Apologists for Evil

July 23, 2009

It's often said, isn't it, that the liberal left is conspicuously silent when it comes to radical Islam, but in my experience that's not entirely true. Many of them are very quick to label anyone who advocates freedom over theocracy as a racist and an Islamophobe.

Indeed, after my last video, where I suggested that we should ban the misogynistic and fascist device known as the burka, I got quite a lot of very angry e-mails from members of the multicultural appeasement lobby; the kind of people who would put their own mothers and daughters in burkas to avoid being called intolerant, and who occupy such high moral ground that you can hardly see them up there through the clouds of self-righteousness.

I'm talking about members of the enlightened liberal intelligentsia that consistently shows itself to be anything but enlightened, or liberal, or intelligent, mainly because it's motivated more by a deep irrational hatred of America than by any real notion of justice or respect, and whose politically correct double standards and cringeworthy cowardice in the face of aggressive Islamism has led many liberal-minded people to actively despise the word "liberal".

You people have certainly reminded me, as if I needed reminding, why my political views have changed in recent years. You see, foolishly perhaps, I used to take freedom for granted, but now, thanks to ultra tolerant self-hating multicultural lemmings like you, I don't.

Politically I always used to be on the liberal left, because I used to believe in social justice, tolerance, respect – you know, the good things in life. I still believe in those things, which is why I'm no longer on the liberal left, because I believe that, in aligning itself, as it has, so completely with the fascism of Islam, and in colluding with an ideology that wants to victimise minorities and kill people for their lifestyle, the liberal left has lost its way, lost its moral authority, and become a threat to our freedom. The medicine has become the disease. And I don't want to be contaminated, so where does that leave me now politically? On the right? No, because that's the last place I want to be. So I suppose it leaves me somewhere in the middle, not knowing which way to turn because my natural constituency has been poisoned by people like you, and I can't tell you how much I resent that. Actually, I probably could, but it might take a while.

Some of you even stooped so low as to try and associate me with an organisation called the BNP, or the British National Party, when everybody who has seen my videos knows full well that my argument is with religion and has got nothing at all to do with race.

I believe the BNP has a racial agenda, and is therefore a racist party, so I would rather vote for nobody at all. In fact I'd rather drive a garden fork through my own foot than vote for the BNP.

But this video is not about them. It's not about right wing fascists. It's about the left wing kind. And I think the word "racist" deserves a public apology for the way it's been hijacked and abused by you multicultural pimps, along with another public apology for all the victims of genuine racism – people who have actually suffered because of the colour of their skin or where they happen to come from, and who can see that word being devalued every time one of you liars uses it to defend a religion, and a fascist religion at that.

Race is irrelevant. We're all one race. That's obvious to anyone with half a brain – we're all part of the same organism. But we're not all one religion, are we? And we're not all one culture. And the truth is, and this is the truth whether you clowns want to hear it or not, that many people in the West feel that we are being invaded (yes, that's the word – invaded) by a religion and a culture whose values we totally reject. Not because we're racists, but because the values themselves are degrading and offensive.

The whole point of female concealment in Islamic society is that men are not expected to take responsibility for their sexual urges, so any woman who is not covered up from head to toe is asking to be raped.

The burka therefore legitimises rape. It apologises for rape. It justifies rape. Are you listening, feminists? And this makes it, in my opinion, as offensive a public statement as a Ku Klux Klan uniform or a Nazi swastika, and I think it should be treated with exactly the same revulsion and contempt.

And as for the free choice argument that you like to defend so disingenuously, well, walking around naked is a free choice, wearing a ski mask into a bank is a free choice, but in neither case would you get away with it for very long.

This so-called choice to wear the burka is exercised more here in the West than it is in Muslim countries because here it's being used quite deliberately as a weapon of cultural jihad, in a naked attempt (if you'll pardon the expression) to undermine the most fundamental of our values, that every human being is born equal.

In Islam, as you may have noticed, every human being is not born equal, not by a long way, and this presents us with a problem in the liberal West, the solution to which is not that we should show how reasonable and tolerant we are by compromising our principles, effectively turning them inside out so as not to cause offence. No, the solution is for Muslim men to start treating women as equals and not as possessions. That's the only solution, it's not negotiable, and saying so doesn't make anybody a racist. Sorry.

As for Islamophobia, just because somebody offends you with their opinion it doesn't give you the right to saddle them with a clinical condition.

There is no such thing as Islamophobia. It simply doesn't exist. And most people now realise just what a cynical manipulative lie that word really is. Suspicion of, or dislike of, Islam is not a phobia. It's an honest, healthy reaction to the evidence that has been provided.

But although Islamophobia doesn't exist, I'll tell you what does exist in great abundance, and that's Islamonausea, in people who are absolutely sick of Islam and its multicultural apologists.

And let's not forget Islamophobianausea. This is nausea brought on by constantly hearing the word Islamophobia. In fact, I've got to stop saying Islamophobia now because I'm already beginning to feel queasy.

These words are being used quite shamelessly to try and engineer an artificial sense of guilt in western society, to redefine our values as prejudices, and to silence legitimate opinion and the free exchange of ideas that have made us what we are and given us our strength. And that's why this is damaging our society in a fundamental way, and it has got to stop.

All over the western world we've become so intimidated into watching every word and thought in case it might offend somebody's precious faith, it's as if the free world has forgotten to inhale.

What happened to our birthright?

We need to take a deep breath. We need to get the oxygen of freedom flowing through our veins again, and through our brains again, and get things back in perspective.

We have nothing to apologise for, and nothing to feel guilty about. And our way of life, despite its many faults (of which we're all very well aware, thank you) is still far superior to anything Islam has to offer, or will ever have to offer, especially if you're female or Jewish or homosexual, or even just a common or garden blasphemer like me.

That is the truth, and most people in the western world realise it's the truth, and there's absolutely nothing wrong with them saying so as loudly and as often as they like.

And you leftie liberal multicultural appeasement monkeys, you're not going to like it, and you're certainly not going to want to speak out for the values that give you the freedom to be the useful idiots you are, but if you could at least find it in your miserable frightened little hearts not to slander those of us who do as racists, we'd all be very grateful.

Peace.

59

The Arrogance of Clergy

October 2, 2009

Although I'm an atheist and a secularist and just about as anti-religion as it's possible to be, I have no problem with anyone believing in God if that's how they want to live their lives. In fact, I think for some people believing in a false god (and this one is false, because they all are) can be quite therapeutic in the way that, say, artificial daylight can help with the winter blues.

But personal faith and public religion are two completely different things. When religion goes public it stops being spiritual and it becomes political, usually running on the moral hypocrisy ticket.

And because it claims divine authority, demanding unconditional submission and obedience from outside the bounds of reason, it despises democracy as much as it despises women and homosexuals (so quite a lot, then) and therefore it's always working towards theocracy, towards strengthening the power and status of clergy.

Public religion exists for the sole benefit of clergy, and clergy exist for the sole benefit of clergy, and this is a pivotal point to understand.

Personal faith, spirituality, whatever you want to call it, doesn't need to be administered and policed by a privileged class of clerical fascists, whereas public religion not only depends on clergy, they depend on it. Neither can exist without the other, and neither is actually necessary.

And they know this, of course, which is why their poxy religion is all about guilt and submission and obedience, not enlightenment. Are you kidding? That's the last thing they want, because enlightened people don't need clergy.

Why do you think the Pope tells Catholics: "Obedience to the doctrine of the Church is the foundation of your faith"? Not the Sermon on the Mount, not loving your neighbour. Obedience is your foundation. Of course it is. It has to be, because the alternative is for you to look into your own heart, and that's the last place these parasites want you looking, because that's where the bullshit detector is.

I've heard clergy referred to as many things – sky pilots, dog-collared vampires, humanity's headlice is one of my favourites – but I don't think those epithets do justice to the true iniquity of the clerical profession, which I believe is engaged in the wilful misdirection of the human race.

Like alchemists who specialise in turning gold into lead, clergy seek to eliminate as much creativity and pleasure as possible, to effectively neutralise the human experience, and to persuade us that this life isn't good enough.

They claim moral authority, when their track record shows that the words "religion" and "moral" don't even belong in the same sentence, any more than the words "creation" and "science", or "Islamic" and "education", or "biblical" and "sense".

In fact, the only moral that any sane person takes from religion is: Don't believe everything you read in books.

And whenever some senior clergyman is quoted in the media, he goes out of his way to portray secular opinion as a form of extremism, when it's they themselves who are the extremists, insisting that we deny the evidence of our own senses, not only to accommodate a raft of unprovable absurdities, but to let them dictate many aspects of our lives. How much more extreme do you want it?

And there are no depths to which these people won't sink to reinforce their crappy dogma.

Condoms, for example. We all know the Catholic Church doesn't like birth control (which is a little odd, as it favours every other form of control) but to knowingly give false information about life and death issues to people who are compelled to obey, as the Pope did a few months ago,* and as Catholic clergy do quite routinely in Africa, is cynical and inhuman, and should be treated as attempted murder.

Every public utterance from a senior clergyman is designed to disempower us and to disconnect us from the planet that gives us life, because they don't want us grounded in any way. So they

---

* In March 2009 the Pope said condoms could make the AIDS crisis in Africa worse. Other Catholic clergy have directly blamed their use for the spread of the disease.

tell us that we don't even belong in this world. We're far too good for this sinful place, because we're sacred and special. Yeah right. We're so special we've got to spend our whole lives on our knees apologising for stuff we had nothing to do with.

Why do you think all the good stuff about religion happens in the future and not in the present? Not at the only point of actual contact you have with reality, and therefore the only point you have any power. That's reserved for prayer and penance and despising the human condition.

Far better, then, for you to focus on that glorious future, and while you're waiting for it to arrive (indeed, while you're waiting for your life to end so that it can arrive) what better moment than the present to get down on your knees and say some prayers and do some penance? (You can never do enough, you know that.)

And while you're down there apologising for your existence as usual, why not take a second to ask yourself a pretty obvious question to me: Who benefits from your faith in the here and now where it actually counts? Who reaps the earthly rewards as opposed to the less tangible heavenly ones in the happy-ever-after land that you've been promised?

Let me ask you something. How many people do you know of who live in a palace? A handful, right? How many of those people are Christian clergymen, and what the bloody hell do you suppose they think they're doing there?

Surely any clergyman who lives in a palace has missed the point and the message of Jesus by a country mile. You don't need to be a theologian to know this. A child could point out that this man hasn't even begun to understand the lesson he's supposed to be teaching others. He's merely acting out a role like a trained monkey. He isn't remotely qualified to hold the position he does, and, in holding it as he does, he debases it and renders it meaningless.

The Archbishop of Canterbury; you remember him, of course. He's the unprincipled quisling who wants sharia law implemented in Britain because it's religious law, and because, for him, religion comes first and people come second. And here in Britain we've become quite used to being lectured by this man about selflessness and non-materialism from the comfort of one of his two magnificent palaces. That's right, two palaces conveniently situated about an hour's drive from each other. I've actually mentioned this before, but I'm having to do it again because I still can't quite believe it myself.

His colleague the Archbishop of York, another media moralist with plenty to say for himself, lives guess where, in a palace. Of course he does. Where else would he live? Anything else would be an insult to Jesus, isn't that right?

And as for the rest of them, the bishops, the archbishops and the cardinals, none of those bastards would dirty their feet on anything less than a mansion.

Of course we all know about the Pope and his massive palace. In fact, he presides over an entire city that doubles as a sovereign state over which he is sole ruler. Nice work if you can get it.

Meanwhile, where are you? Still on your knees praying for salvation, by any chance? Well, if so, keep it up, because your favourite televangelist needs to buy himself a new private jet with your money – in Jesus' name, of course.

That Jesus, he's going to be a very wealthy young man if he ever comes back, isn't he, with all that stuff that's been bought in his name. All that crude extravagant unnecessary luxury.

I wonder what he'll think when he realises that the image of his grisly death on the cross has been turned into the most lucrative money-grubbing logo in human history and that two thousand years on it's still raking in mountains of cold hard cash, mostly from poor people.

I wonder if Jesus will allow himself a twinge of conscience, and reflect that perhaps he is the one who should be repenting, and not us. And that it's he who should be asking our forgiveness for allowing his name to be hijacked and exploited by these cynical life-sucking criminals. I guess we'll just have to wait and see.

In the meantime, turn to religion if you really have to for comfort, if it's all you've got to lean on. But, whatever you do, don't turn to religion for the truth. Religion doesn't know the truth, and these men are living proof of that. If, by some miracle, they were to stumble upon the truth, they would hide it to protect their stinking dogma the way it protects them.

How obvious does it have to be that these are not men of humility and wisdom (which is kind of the Jesus model, and really what we were looking for) but career politicians. Petty, small-minded, status-obsessed, ego-bound men. What a humiliating state for anyone claiming to be a spiritual teacher. The very pharisees, in fact, that Jesus himself resisted. The ones obsessed with their own importance, their own grandiosity, with the status quo at any cost, with dogma over compassion every single time.

The ones who behave as if people exist for the benefit of religion and not the other way round.

I found out recently that the word heretic comes from the Greek word *hairetikos*, meaning able to choose, which pretty much says it all, don't you think? Peace, and God bless atheism.

60

Wake Up, America

October 22, 2009

You remember the cartel of Islamic dictatorships that hijacked the United Nations Human Rights Council, don't you? And then promptly passed a resolution banning criticism of religion? Yes, of course you do.

Well, apparently they've decided now that the Universal Declaration of Human Rights gives people just a bit too much freedom and dignity for their liking, so they've devised their own Islamic human rights charter – which is a bit like Satan getting his own set of pearly gates, and about as convincing.

Unfortunately the Islamic charter is based on sharia, which is, of course, invalid because it's God's law, and God doesn't exist.

To claim that he does is extremely offensive to those of us who passionately believe otherwise. It's a grave insult to our most deeply cherished beliefs, an assault on the very core of our being, no less, and a violation, therefore, of our human rights, isn't it? Well, isn't it?

Now all this would be something of a tiresome joke, if not for the fact that this nonsense is beginning to have a real effect on our basic freedoms, certainly here in Europe, and Americans would do well to wake up and pay attention to what's going on.

Ever since the Islamic countries demanded that western governments make it a crime to criticise Islam, all over Europe blasphemy laws and religious insult laws are being used to criminalise freedom of speech.

The latest is Ireland, a country that has been literally raped by religion, yet has passed a law protecting it from criticism. Talk about Stockholm Syndrome.

Free speech, they tell us, carries certain responsibilities. Too true it does, the primary one being that what you say should be the truth.

And the truth should never be embarrassing, and it should never be illegal, and any government that is so embarrassed by the truth that it makes it illegal is governing under false pretences.

The Dutch government, for example, which is in the process of embarrassing itself by prosecuting the leader of one of the country's largest political parties, for the crime of telling the truth.

You see, these days in Europe we've become so used to weasel words and double standards that the truth has become distinctly unfashionable. Speaking your mind is now seen as virtually anti-social because some opportunistic crybaby is sure to take offence and throw a tantrum, and that might threaten "community cohesion".

Now what has all this got to do with America? Well, President

Obama is very keen on showing respect to the Muslim world, and nobody can fault him on his record so far, bowing, as he did, to the king of Saudi Arabia like some kind of vassal, and then making a rather flattering, some might even say dishonest speech in Cairo – although to be fair he did stop short of prostrating himself towards Mecca, at least for the time being.

But because he wants to play ball with Islam (especially now they've given him a peace prize through their shills in the Norwegian establishment that he's going to have to justify for the next three years – the Iranians must be rubbing their hands with glee at that one) the American government has now done something that, if they did it in their own country, it would violate the Constitution. They've co-sponsored a UN resolution that puts a limit on freedom of speech, because the Islamic countries don't like free speech. They don't like free anything, except free foreign aid, obviously. They can't get enough of that.

Even the Saudis want aid now. Have you heard the latest? I could hardly believe it. The Saudis have said that when the world starts using less oil they expect to be compensated for loss of income. You really couldn't make it up, could you?

The problem with the new touchy-feely American administration is not that it wants to be friendly and respectful to everyone; that's very laudable. It's just that when you have a moral agenda like that it can be tempting to cut corners, especially when it comes to inconvenient things like constitutional amendments.

And if they're doing this now outside the United States where they can get away with it, it's only a matter of time before this is allowed to become international law, and then you know they'll start trying to do it inside the United States as well, in the name of "community cohesion". Get used to that phrase, America. It's coming your way.

And this matters. It matters a lot, not only to Americans but to all of us who see the American Constitution as the anchor for western civilisation – which is what it is.

We know that no matter how spineless our politicians are in Europe and elsewhere (and here in Europe they've barely got a vertebra between them) as long as America's First Amendment remains inviolate there will always be an oasis of freedom on this planet that Islam cannot touch. But as soon as anyone is allowed to interfere with it, to water it down, to reinterpret, to chip and chisel away at the First Amendment for reasons of religious or cultural sensitivity, then we can wave our civilisation goodbye.

Americans voted for change at the last election. They didn't vote for surrender.

Watch what's happening in Europe, America. Cherish that Constitution, and don't let Islam anywhere near it, for all our sakes.

Remember the words of Mr Omar Ahmad, co-founder of the Council on American-Islamic Relations, who said that Islam is not in America to be equal to other faiths, but to become dominant, and that the Koran should be the highest authority in America. That'll be higher than the Constitution, then, by my reckoning.

If President Obama is serious about showing respect to the Muslim world then he should pay them the compliment of telling them the truth, that their religion is entitled to as much respect as it gives – zero; that, with their record, no Islamic country has any business even holding an opinion on human rights, let alone serving on a legislative body; that asking the people of the free world to compromise their fundamental values is far, far more insulting than any set of cartoons or any book could ever be; and that if the Islamic countries had an ounce of genuine honour between them they would issue a full and unconditional apology.

That's what he should say because it's the truth. Everyone in the free world knows it's the truth, so let's hope the truth becomes fashionable again before too long.

Peace. Oh yes.

11775872R0017

Made in the USA
Lexington, KY
31 October 2011